Dorys Crow Grovee

Frank & Susan Redmond

T. S. ELIOT

A Symposium for his seventieth birthday

Aprilisthecruelstmthbreedng Lilacsoutofthedeadland
NAM·SIBYLLAM
QVIDEM·CVMIS
EGO·IPSE·OCVLIS
MEIS·VIDI·IN
AMPVLLA·PENDERE
ET·CVM·ILLI·PVERI
DICERENT
ΣΙΒΥΛΛΑ·ΤΙ·ΘΕΛΕΙΣ
RESPONDEBAT·ILLA
ΑΠΟΘΑΝΕΙΝ·ΘΕΛΩ.
LA·TERRE·GASTE·ET·SOUTAINE
NAC·ANIVEIL·NA·MWG·NA·DYN
ne·in·the·watir·no·fyssh. Dauid me fecit Thomae

T. S. ELIOT

A SYMPOSIUM FOR HIS SEVENTIETH BIRTHDAY

EDITED BY

NEVILLE BRAYBROOKE

NEW YORK
FARRAR, STRAUS & CUDAHY
1958

Library of Congress catalog card number 58—11939

PRINTED AND BOUND IN ENGLAND BY
HAZELL WATSON AND VINEY LTD
AYLESBURY AND SLOUGH

Contents

Acknowledgements

I SHOULD like to thank many Headmasters and Headmistresses and their staffs for their ready help in making possible the school section to be found on pp. 104–118. I should also like to thank Mr L. P. Hartley for acting as 'a go-between' and writing an introductory piece to this section. I am most grateful, too, for help and advice from Mr Vincent Cronin, Mr W. F. Jackson Knight and Mr John S. Landels.

The quotations from Mr Eliot's work are reprinted by kind permission of Messrs Faber & Faber Ltd.

Introduction

. . . nothing matters but the quality
of the affection—
in the end—that has carved the trace in the mind . . .

EZRA POUND

BIRTHDAYS are a time of celebration. As the years slip into the past, so different memories stir—a friend crossing the Luxembourg Gardens waving a branch of lilac; the cry of quail over the New England coast; the chattering teeth of a Persian cat stalking his prey across the green fields of Russell Square. The traditional iced cake, so eagerly anticipated when young, comes to acquire a fresh significance—a sign for giving thanks for what has gone before; again, even the number of candles acquire a new meaning—often at the rate of one a decade, or seven for seventy: the three score years and ten of life now serve to recall the age of reason, a nursery tea in St Louis and perhaps the attendant figures of Cousins Nancy and Harriet, or a maiden aunt with her four servants, dogs and favourite parrot. 'The beginning shall remind us of the end.' For on 26 September 1888, a seventh child was born to Charlotte Chauncy Stearns and Henry Ware Eliot: this child they had christened Thomas, and by the Christian calendar September 26 marks the double feast of the saints and martyrs, Cyprian and Justina. There may be a sense, too, in which saints, no less than angels, may be called 'guardians'.

In the Third Century the Empress Eudocia wrote a poem running to three books, celebrating the lives of Cyprian, surnamed the Magician, and Justina, a beautiful maiden of Antioch. These books have been lost, but Photius, a scribe of the period, has sent report after him of the poem's wonderful merits and has himself offered a prose abstract of it. According to this version, Cyprian travelled widely—from Athens and the parts about Mount Olympus in Macedonia to

Argos, Phrygia, and Memphis in Egypt; from Chaldaea to the Indies; and everywhere his quest was the same—the pursuit of the black arts of sorcery. After one such journey, a friend invoked his aid: this nobleman had desired passionately for some months to win Justina, but she, having secretly dedicated herself to God, refused his every advance. Now he wished to bring her into subjection by any means. In a word, could not a spell be cast? So Cyprian agreed, and summoning up his dark spirits was bewildered when she remained quite unaffected by their presence; he began to believe that she was protected by legions of spirits more powerful than his own, and his curiosity was aroused. On a Sunday following, therefore, under the guidance of a learned and holy priest, he visited a community of Christians: '[There], I saw a choir of Heaven's men, or of angels, singing to God, adding at the end of every verse in the psalms the Hebrew refrain "Alleluia", so that they seemed not to be men [of this earth].' Soon his conversion followed and from being the lay-sweeper of a church in the diocese he rose to being the Bishop of Antioch. However, coinciding with this episcopal appointment, another wave of persecution broke out and by another coincidence he found himself condemned to stand trial at Damascus before the same judge as Justina: she was ordered to be whipped and he was also whipped—though in his case steel barbs were ordered to be fixed to the ropes. Then, chained together, they were led before Dioclesian who demanded their instant death, which was carried out on the banks of the river Gallus. In Rome, their relics can be seen in the Basilica of St John Lateran, the most ancient church in Christendom.

Strictly speaking, this third-century tale has no direct bearing on Thomas Stearns Eliot—save that it does connect with the writings of a third-century mystic and contemporary of St Cyprian and St Justina—namely, St Gregory of Nyssa, whose ideas (as Mr Raymond Preston suggests on another page) seem to have influenced certain sections of the *Four Quartets*. This is an example of what another contributor, a Polish girl of eighteen, calls 'chain-reaction in poetry'. For the story of the martyrs has echoes.

Justina is as much a prototype of Celia Coplestone, as Harry,

Lord Monchensey, is a potential Charles de Foucauld who also seeks:

> the worship in the desert, the thirst and deprivation,
> A stony sanctuary and a primitive altar,
> The heat of the sun and the icy vigil,
> A care over lives of humble people,
> The lesson of ignorance, of incurable diseases.

So ends one of the closing speeches of Scene II, Act II, in *The Family Reunion*, whilst, in the closing minutes of *The Cocktail Party*, Sir Henry Harcourt-Reilly asks:

> Do you imagine that the Saint in the desert
> With spiritual evil always at his shoulder
> Suffered any less from hunger, damp, exposure,
> Bowel trouble, and fears of lions,
> Cold of the night, and heat of the day, than we should?

If in 1939 Harry's new life left a certain ambiguity in an audience's mind about exactly what course he was going to follow on leaving Wishwood, then in 1949 it would seem that in the later play the dramatist was absolutely determined that there should be no similar misgivings about the path that Celia chose, nor the kind of martyrdom to which it led in the island of Kinkanja—'crucifixion' and, as a practical geographical afterthought, 'very near an ant hill'. In the case of Lord Monchensey there is an echo from the life of Charles Eugène, Vicomte de Foucauld, whose biography by René Bazin Mr Eliot appears to have read, whereas with Justina and Celia Coplestone something less conscious has been at work—not quite race-memory, but rather more a clearing away for the bones of revelation to discover the traces in the mind, a developing attributed by some to the history of chance, by others to the intervention of the Fates or 'guardians' of Divine Providence. And this territory of echo, race-memory and providence is one that Mr Eliot has particularly made his own.

Answering for myself, I would say that here lies much of his significance . . . although, before I further this point, I should like to add that it has been one of my aims in editing this symposium that members of every generation should answer this question for themselves. Which is why, in order to make the picture as complete as possible, I approached over a hundred headmasters and headmistresses during 1957, so that a short selection of the views of boys and girls might be included.

It is sometimes argued by those who teach that there are very few themes for plays: the Classical Greek drama, or the works of Shakespeare, provide ready examples of what they mean. Accordingly, since plots are so limited, it follows that echoes are never hard to catch; it might even be argued that appreciation goes by comparison—that the *Ion* of Euripides and the operas of Gilbert and Sullivan lead to a fuller appreciation of *The Confidential Clerk*, or that through Mrs Shuttlethwaite Lady Elizabeth Mulhammer can trace a mixed ancestry to Lady Bracknell and Millamant. 'My words echo,' the poet once wrote—and every echo lends greater volume to what has sounded before, whether on the shores of Asia, from the heights of Mount Olympus, or along the grey wastes of Edgware Road. Lucasta Angel is described by Sir Claude Mulhammer's trusted Eggerson as 'rather flighty', which is a more sophisticated form of punning than calling a drunken knight Sir Toby Belch. For poets, no less than their poems, seldom speak consecutively, since what they say consists largely in suggesting many different things at one and the same time; and, at these most heightened moments, their words will stir, jostle and break open, revealing unsuspected patterns. The beginning leads to the end, and *vice versa*; ascending becomes descending and the way forward is the way back. The cat that is an instrument to learn benevolence upon is transformed into Christ the Tiger—a quick change from Christopher Smart's *Song of David* to T. S. Eliot's *Gerontion*; or Old Possum's Mungojerrie and Rumpleteazer slinking along Launceston Place may recall the yellow fog that rubs its back upon the window-panes in *Prufrock*. Mr Eliot may write humorously on 'the Naming of Cats', but the choosing of any name has always been for him a most careful procedure; a reader should not forget that his first book of poems from the Egotist Press carried the full title of *Prufrock and Other Observations*. For example, it is difficult to think of the great Bela Szogody and his film company Pan-Am-Eagle as fictions; they are observed with the precise degree of reality that smacks of authenticity, like the island of Kinkanja in the same play. Yet a phrase following the immediate naming of that island, 'an island that you won't have heard of yet', led me to approach the London Royal Geographical Society: the assistant Map Curator replied that their gazetteers did not disclose any island in the world 'by the name of Kinkanja'.

Again, a line such as 'Now that lilacs are in bloom' may remind one critic of Whitman's 'When Lilacs Last in the Dooryard Bloom'd' or another of Rupert Brooke's 'Grantchester' poem, or, if either happens to be a literary detective, then 'lilac' may act as a clue sending them off to the Luxembourg Gardens where a friend once greeted the poet with a branch, a friend later 'mixed in the mud at Gallipoli', and whose memory was touched off by reading Henri Massis's *Evocations* three years after it had appeared in Paris—all of which can be tracked down to the Editor's Commentary in Volume XIII, Number LII, of the *Criterion* for April 1934. Similarly, for those of a younger generation, that 'lilac' line from *A Portrait of a Lady* may evoke the music of Ivor Novello, which in turn may lead to a comparison between the music-hall rhythms of *Sweeney Agonistes* ('*Under the bamboo*') and the plain-chant rhythms employed in his 'book of words' for his pageant, *The Rock* ('O Light Invisible, we praise Thee'). Indeed, Mr Eliot's later work has shown a most successful fusion of both strains, sacred and profane.

In the poet's middle years, the 1930 *Ash-Wednesday* period, extreme complexity often punctuated extreme simplicity:

> Because I do not hope to turn again
> Because I do not hope
> Because I do not hope to turn . . .

These opening lines carry on 'the prickly pear' nursery music of *The Hollow Men* of 1925; and yet, almost imperceptibly, the rhythm has altered, acquiring as it were an underlying note of litany. In the earlier poem '*For thine is the Kingdom*' remained a stifled, interrupted, half-broken refrain—to which a corollary was now hinted: 'Verily I say unto you, Except ye be converted, and become as little children, ye shall not enter into the Kingdom. . . .' So at least might run a religious interpretation. Another, on a more literal level, might attribute the lines to children spinning themselves like tops in London squares until dizzy with their own turning they tumble on the grass. For *Ash-Wednesday* (or *Salutation* as part of it was first published—a title emphasizing in part its inherent Marian theme) shows once more in its opening lines a preoccupation that has been with Mr Eliot from the start—a feeling for children and a return to Eden; an anticipation of second childhood and a return from Eden: in short, innocence the wiser for experience and yet none the less innocent for that experience. In this paradox of Christianity the apple-tree acts as a symbol, and it is worth remembering that when children are young they have about them the freshness of apples. The village of Little Gidding with its

> children in the apple-tree
> Not known, because not looked for

links with Burnt Norton, the Gloucestershire house in which the poet discovered that 'the leaves were full of children', a reminder of even earlier still when in New Hampshire he had also heard 'children's voices in the orchard' as he stood listening and watching:

> Golden head, black wing,
> Cling, swing,
> Spring, sing,
> Swing up into the apple-tree.

Poetically, in this backward chronology from *Little Gidding* to 'New Hampshire', the Atlantic has been crossed, just as one day in 1637 a cordwainer called Andrew Eliot in actual fact left East Coker to make this fifty-day sea-voyage, becoming subsequently enrolled as a member of the First Church of Beverley, Massachusetts, in 1670; then three centuries later one of his descendants returned to this Somerset village to bring it immortal fame in his verse. These are journeys in time, journeys that biographers, critics and literary historians pursue haltingly; at the best they can no more than retrace, lead or point—each according to his vision, time and background. Ultimately many of their deductions will remain guesswork, since they will be marked by the flaws of their own natures—excess and prejudice of judgment, or limited understanding. In trying to arrive at the whole truth, they will reach only part of the truth—a maxim as humbling for the critic to remember as for an audience to be told: 'Human kind cannot bear very much reality.' Moreover, Archbishop Becket's warning appeared repeated word for word in *Burnt Norton*—a repetition doubtless intended to banish any idea that an author's character was speaking merely to a supposed Chorus of Women of Canterbury in 1170, but intended to reinforce that the author himself was addressing an audience of listeners as active participants, not spectators, in a drama of all time. 'And all is always now.'

In his poetry and his plays, with remarkable consistency, Mr Eliot has developed many of the religious, sociological and political themes that he has outlined in his critical essays, primers of modern heresy, and notes towards definition. 'All argument is basically theological' is another maxim from another devout churchman of another century that matches his own approach. Likewise, his concern for the use of criticism has been a concern for life, since criticism reflects life—and in life guesses have to be made. A major critic in literature needs the same kind of luck as attends a general in battle—and in each his lucky guessing may be said to comprise a part of his talent. 'The gods smiled kindly' was a frequent epithet on Classical heroes, which might be interpreted in the present Age of Psychology as the conspiring together of coincidence with potentiality, or the synchronizing of providence with capability. Or it might simply be said, in Mr Eliot's view, that nothing is ever fortuitous.

In the third part of *East Coker* an image from the third part of *Burnt Norton* is repeated—memories of the tube, or underground trains that wait too long; and here those who know their London may well recall that Mr Eliot lived for many years in a flat near the Thames, one of whose nearest stations was South Kensington, a station famous for delays since drivers frequently put in time here so as to get back to schedule—a factor perhaps causing those merchant bankers, distinguished civil servants and chairmen of many committees to let a few fancies, empty of meaning, 'flicker over [their] strained time-ridden faces'. Further, those who remember the year of the poem's composition will remember that it coincided with the

Blitzkrieg, a period during which the tubes would fill nightly with Londoners, among them old women like wizened apples clutching at the folds of their shawls. And so from the apples of age back to the apple-time of youth, or from the apple-tree of Paradise to the apple-tree (recalled in *Little Gidding*) that made Redemption possible.

Mr Eliot the publisher travelling to work, Mr Eliot the Air Raid Warden—both aspects have met in Mr Eliot the poet of the *Four Quartets*; and the sudden shifts and changes of meaning in these Quartets have been achieved partly by conscious memory and the setting down of experience, partly by means of echo and an unconscious tapping of race-memory. To return to the apple-tree, Mr Eliot may have had in the back of his mind the comparison drawn by St John of the Cross (after all, he paraphrases five lines direct from the *Ascent of Mount Carmel* in *East Coker*), or it may simply be that there is in man a memory so strong that the branches of a tree, however faintly, cannot fail to stir with the voices of Eden, or with the scene enacted upon a small hill in Palestine some nineteen hundred years ago. Indeed, Mr Eliot's own publishing house, more than any other, has always been conspicuous in issuing books that explore this particular territory, whilst he himself, more than any other living poet, has written phrases whose familiar repetition has turned them into the accepted catchphrases of contemporary speech: 'I have measured out my life with coffee spoons', 'I shall wear the bottoms of my trousers rolled'—or a plain statement such as, 'No! I am not Prince Hamlet, nor was not meant to be'. All these come from *The Love Song of J. Alfred Prufrock* and have in the last forty years achieved a fame so wide that they frequently appear as newspaper captions without acknowledgement. Numerous novels, too, have taken their titles from his lines—for instance, *A Handful of Dust* by Evelyn Waugh in the 'thirties and *The Mango on the Mango Tree* by David Mathew in the 'forties—or now in the present decade, with a hint of parody, *Ash on a Young Man's Sleeve* by Dannie Abse. Equally successfully has the poet brought to life the words of others: 'Sweet Thames, run softly', 'A cold coming'—or his translation of the motto of Mary Queen of Scots into, 'In my beginning is my end'. To be more personal, I might add that when I began to plan this essay I was staying in Belgium. Every evening walking along by the quay-side cafés of the Scheldt—the 'Bingo', 'Marina' and 'Cheerio'—I found myself repeating the line from *Gerontion*, 'Spawned in some estaminet of Antwerp', just as I remember Irish schoolboys muttering fragments from the *Credo* during rugger matches. Similarly, the snatches of music-hall songs will as readily be learnt by heart as the great speeches of tragedy: Marie Lloyd singing 'My Old Man', or an actor delivering the soliloquy, 'Tomorrow and tomorrow and to-morrow. . . .' And between these two levels, what a brilliant tele-scoping lies in this telegram from *The Waste Land*: 'O O O O that Shakespeherian Rag. . . .'

'In a play of Shakespeare you get several levels'—and Mr Eliot in his famous essay on 'The Use of Poetry' went on to list them: plot; character and conflict of character; language and phrasing; rhythm; 'and for auditors of greater sensitiveness and understanding a meaning which reveals itself gradually'. Naturally, too, the appeal exerted by certain plays has altered with certain periods. Obviously it would be in the interests of astute theatrical enterprise to put on *Henry VIII* during Coronation festivities, as the Old Vic did in 1953. But putting aside such eventualities, it must also be said that certain plays more than others have fired the audiences of certain periods. It seems that *Antony and Cleopatra* especially appealed to the Renaissance public, *Hamlet* especially to followers of the Romantic Movement and *Coriolanus* especially to those who lived in the years *entre deux guerres*. Yet I think there are dangers of over simplification in linking Mr Eliot's 'Triumphal March' (1931) and 'Difficulties of a Statesman' (1932) too closely with the period of their composition, since even before 1920 in 'A Cooking Egg' he had already coupled 'Sydney and Coriolanus', while in 'Ode', an early poem from *The Harvard Advocate* of 24 June 1910 (and subsequently reprinted only in Mr Eliot's limited-edition from the Ovid Press in 1920, *Ara Vos Pec*), he had chosen this epigraph from Act IV, Scene V of the Shakespearean play:

> My name is Caius Marcus, who hath done
> To thee particularly, and to all the Volsces
> Great hurt and mischief.

When therefore in *The Waste Land* in 1922 he revived memories 'for a moment of a broken Coriolanus', he was simply repeating a theme which had already begun to catch his imagination a decade before.

In 'Triumphal March' and 'Difficulties of a Statesman', launched in the 'thirties under the general title of *Coriolan* poems—a series intended to run to four, but stopping at two—the attitude presented was not so much one of open disgust at Fascism and the spread of Nazism, but something more profoundly experienced: the eagles in the march-past may be German, but a reference to 'the temple' suggests an ambiguity—they may be Roman, since the concern of these *Coriolan* poems lies with the basic problem of the relationship between the individual and the state—a problem in any civilization, but a problem particularly accentuated in the 'thirties by the rise of a Fuehrer and an increase in dictatorship in Italy. Nowadays, scapegoats such as Hitler with his attendant anti-Semitism and Mussolini with his racial discrimination, are harder to seize upon; it may also be that atomic warfare offers no real protection other than a state of grace—which, if it is so, to this extent makes the basic problem for today not so much one between the individual and the state, but rather one between the individual and the state of his soul. It is the age-old Christian problem: 'Render therefore unto Caesar the things that are Caesar's; and unto God the things that are God's.' In the transition from the 'thirties to the 'fifties, from an Era of Social Realism to an Age of Psychology, so much has the need changed from social to spiritual alleviation that psychiatrists in clinics run by the state now refer to the act of taking the burden of guilt off their patients' shoulders as an act of personal transference: a character like Sir Henry Harcourt-Reilly would doubtless call such guilt the burden of original sin—and certainly, in psychological terms, it might be argued that the greatest act of transference in recorded history took place on a Cross. Moreover, it should be remembered that Christ was born into a Jewish society, which was also a patriarchy, and that psychiatry is based on patriarchal principles—a Jewish inheritance that persists, as in the Christian religion, whatever the actual birth of its practitioners. In an Age of Psychology, with the emphasis on personal guilt growing together with a sense of sin returning,

Measure for Measure appears to have achieved a significance in repertory and amateur theatricals reminiscent of *Coriolanus* twenty years ago.

In *The Cocktail Party* Mrs Chamberlayne is asked to believe that when the Unidentified Guest first saw Celia Coplestone, he saw an image,

> standing behind [the] chair,
> Of a Celia Coplestone whose face showed the astonishment
> Of the first five minutes after a violent death.

In *Measure for Measure*, the Duke of Vienna says of Angelo:

> There is a kind of character in thy life,
> That to the observer doth thy history
> Fully unfold.

The areas are similar—an exploration of which was continued in *The Confidential Clerk*. Here again the play was strictly neither tragedy nor comedy, but a mixture: at the end all ended reasonably well. The curtain fell on *reasonably*—perhaps the best that could be expected of imperfect players on an imperfect stage. But now came the moments after, the moments whether consciously or not that are always so important with Mr Eliot's work. Something very close to a West End comedy had been enjoyed; but this might be part of an illusion, since if an audience's reaction to Angelo might be 'What a hypocrite!' then to Mulhammer, and to a lesser degree to the others, they might think themselves not so unalike, and in thinking this come to see themselves with the eyes of their own consciences. It is as well to remember that Mr Eliot asks for participants, not spectators, in his theatre: 'Judge not that ye be not judged. For with what judgment ye judge, ye shall be judged: and with what measure ye mete, it shall be measured to you again.' The part of the Duke in *Measure for Measure* acts like a commentary on this text, just as rather less successfully Mr Eliot imitated his blessing 'Peace be with you', when he put into the mouth of Sir Henry the impossibly difficult, 'Go in peace. And work out your salvation with diligence'. After all, *Gerontion* was headed with words taken from the Duke, and Mr Eliot as a critic has revealed a most penetrating knowledge of the inner workings of this tragi-comedy, and Claudio's famous speech beginning 'Ay, but to die, and go we know not where' leads on to his natural fears about being

> blown with restless violence round about
> The pendent world,

a fear re-echoed by Gerontion in 'his after-dinner sleep' when he sees his friends being

> whirled
> Beyond the circuit of the shuddering Bear
> In fractured atoms.

Yet what was forced in *The Cocktail Party* (such as the libation scene) had been smoothed away in the next play, so that no longer was there any obvious preaching. Some reviewers went so far as to label *The Confidential Clerk* as a farce of mistaken identity; and as far as they went they were right, but it was also a play presenting the search for a father figure—psychologically, spiritually and in actual fact.

> All I wanted was relief
> From the nagging annoyance of knowing there's a fact
> That one doesn't know. But the fact itself
> Is unimportant, once one knows it.

Sir Claude in his quest has abandoned being a potter, preferring to be a financier; for him, an interest in ceramics takes the place of religion. 'The potter . . . maketh both vessels that are for clean uses, and likewise such as serve to the contrary: but what is the use of these vessels, the potter is to judge.' Through the others, he has to learn to judge, and especially through Colby, that as he was not only mistaken about the boy's heredity, so too was he mistaken to steer him away from a musical career to one in the City, even if loyalty to his vocation would have advanced him no further than an organist's stool in Joshua Park. 'Know thyself,' said the Delphic Oracle; 'To thine ownself be true,' said Shakespeare; and between these exhortations come Christ's two teachings, 'Be the children of your Father which is in heaven' and 'I say unto you, Whosoever shall not receive the kingdom of God as a little child shall in no wise enter therein'. In rapid succession I have quoted the parable of the potter from the *Book of Wisdom* and from the Gospels of St Matthew and St Luke. Mr Eliot's style has been very much influenced by the Bible, especially the Authorized Version—and it might be added not only his style, but his entire manner of thinking.

The drama of the Church he has interpreted through the stage. In 'Triumphal March' there is the child Cyril who confuses the offertory bell of the Mass with that of a street-crier, just as when the Dowager Lady Monchensey says to the parlourmaid in *The Family Reunion*, 'Not yet! I will ring for you', there may be in this opening line of the play a distant reminder of a server crossing an altar. Mr Eliot has declared elsewhere that 'the consummation of the drama, the perfect and ideal drama, is to be found in the ceremony of the Mass'. For as the drama moved from the steps of the altar to the steps of the church and from thence to a platform in the market-place, so always present in the larger drama of life there will be present these echoes of that religious beginning and perhaps even earlier still of rituals practised long before the birth of Christianity. Tiger Rag—and Christ the Tiger, the singers of Israel—and the crooners of Manhattan: here is a brief history of psalms and hymns in telegraphic style. Or there are the swear-words and blasphemies of any crowd—be the heroes the golf-club Captains or soldiers of any Imperial army—whose shouts and ejaculations in reverse may have their counterpart in the litanies of the saints and emphasize how constant is the need for men to live by some form of incantation, however profane. '*Crumpets*' shouts 'young Cyril' when he hears the bell in church on Easter Day, a word that carries in its context a double meaning of profanity and childish innocence, an irony further marked by the linking of sex and religion with spring-rites and the Church's incorporation of those most early primitive rites into her own rituals. Again, Cyril's interruption is followed by his parents' colloquialism, 'Give us a light', followed by a double repetition of the one-word line, 'Light'—a two-way play on meaning suggesting an ordinary human request and at the same time perhaps an unconscious prayer for help. And back in this territory it might be asked to what extent, consciously or unconsciously, did the poet's first name incline him to choose another of that name for the chief character of his first play, *Murder in the Cathedral*?

The question points back to two other saints who were martyrs, Cyprian and Justina—the point at which this excursion into echo, race-memory and providence began. Of course, there are many other approaches to the work of T. S. Eliot, and not all the arguments in this book will prove necessarily consistent, since rather than run the risk of Christian discrimination, I invited non-believers as well as believers to contribute. Nor did I ask any to withhold their disagreements or differences of opinion, since that would have been offensive to truth; and, again, about half my team are under thirty-five. Naturally, there are many others whose names are intimately connected with that of T. S. Eliot, but here I have tried in particular to gather those who have had a practical experience of his work—actors and actresses; stage, film and television producers; composers and school-teachers. I have also chosen others who have achieved eminence in the world of letters, but who have not had the chance to express their appreciation in previous symposiums and birthday volumes. This accounts for the omission of many distinguished poets and critics. A gap, which I noticed in these previous books, were studies of Mr Eliot as a translator and classical scholar as well as a moral and political writer: Mr Vincent Cronin, Mr Jackson Knight, Miss Iris Murdoch and Mr J. M. Cameron now redress the balance. I had hoped, too, to have something from an illustrator's point of view. But Miss Gertrude Hermes, whose illustration graced the Ariel edition of *Animula*, replied: 'I am afraid words are not my medium at all. I do not remember what my approach to the poem was, except that it was very exciting to be asked to make engravings for such a lovely poem.' A fair enough reason. Miss Harriet Shaw Weaver, whom I also approached for a possible memoir of the early *Egotist* days, prayed to hold herself excused, being 'twelve years older than Mr Eliot, to the month'. A reason that gallantry could not fail to respect. Yet if there were disappointments on the way—the sad deaths of Wyndham Lewis, Roy Campbell and Middleton Murry—there were last-minute rewards: the epigraph from *The Waste Land* in the beautiful lettering of Mr David Jones, a birthday poem from Mr Charles Causley a week before handing the anthology in and the sudden arrival of a detailed analysis of *The Cultivation of Christmas Trees*, Mr Eliot's last poem to appear before this book went to press.

And now one generalization or final impression. In my six months' gathering, never before have I received so many postcards with instructions to change the order of sentences, delete phrases or substitute new ones; never before have I been asked by so many authors to return their manuscripts for revisions, second thoughts or re-writings. 'Mr Eliot has made me more conscious of my words than any other living writer,' said one on the telephone. I was reminded for an instant of the superb stage measure achieved in Act II of *The Confidential Clerk*, the clearing away of all unnecessary dead verbiage—a task at which Mr Eliot has worked so diligently in all his prose and poetry for close on half a century. I was reminded of Mr Eliot's own dictum that when language becomes new once more, that is one of the most important things that can happen to a nation. Perhaps much more than seventy years are celebrated in this book.

Three Poems

Ode

Since the human motive is always fallible
And the design of good
Draws from none but the humble
Such a life as is always new,

May you, sifting truly the power of fantasy
Over the growing child,
Kindling time like a candle,
Marvel, seeing its praise transformed.

Warn mankind, though softly: 'Time remains plausible.
Test the contented man;
Seek within his responses,
And in yours, what must still be found.'

Since the self-corrected alone is innocent
And the impulsive heart
Brings betrayal of glory,
Nor can thrive till it live by prayer,

Who can better teach how little is visible
Save in the eye of God?
Tentatively you struggled,
Mapping slowly the land we know.

Not by wide acclaim you tested accomplishment.
Early fame was deceit;
Failures nourished the honest,
Moulded still by a force unknown.

Rich in time's ambition, you yet chose penury,
Paying a timeless debt,
One intensity binding
Future ages and all the Past.

Next you pruned the English language of luxury
Lest it should waste its strength,
Matching strictness to music,
Incantation to living speech.

Art is various, verse develops unsearchably.
See, from the mid-leaf born,
Growth may copy the cactus,
Yet adhere to its ancient root.

Prayer alone makes all that perishes permanent.
Step by step we are led
Past a moment of terror:
From that moment our works proceed.

These things came to you as you waited patiently
Under the tree of life.
Taking Dante for master,
You descanted on London Bridge.

Many streets and lives we judge by that instrument,
Yet no measurement can
Judge the loss of a person,
So discreet is the dance of life.

Let none doubt the disguise. See how deformity
Under attentive eyes
Bears perfection within it,
Speaking low its athletic style.

Strong is he who knows mankind through infirmity
And who practises love,
Seeing each from the godhead
Living here as an earthly son.

This, then, most, your birthday justly will celebrate,
That the divining mind
Finds regenerate waters
Turning all to effects of grace.

Fountain cities, too, preserve a community
Never entirely lost
Though destruction, though bondage
Leave their mark on the roads and walls.

Vision gives man strength no danger will dominate.
Time is redeemed, while he
Earths in safety the lightning
Shining through the ironic mask.

How best keep the bold example in memory?
Age is potent to show
Youth's impelled emulation
How to feed its exalted will.

Each for all men's hearts is counted responsible.
Therefore that land is waste
Which forgets for a moment
Passion's healer and treasured spring.

VERNON WATKINS

Fall-out Over Heaven

'I'll show you fear in a handful of dust.'
(*The Waste Land*)

'And dust shall be the serpent's meat.'
(*Isaiah:* lxv. 25)

The atom, broken in the shell,
Licks up Eden's reach, and Hell.

To Adam back his rib is thrown;
A mole of woman quakes, undone.

From the ground the knife of Cain
Slays the brother it has slain.

To Moses' empty gorge, like smoke
Rush backward all the words he spoke.

Lucifer roars up from earth.
Down falls Christ into his death. . . .

'She, supposing him to be the gardener . . .'
(*John:* xx. 15)

DJUNA BARNES

Down by the Riverside . . .

Down by the riverside the grass grows deep,
Seventy branches tiger-stripe my sheep,
And where the Tamar turns her watery fan
I search its city for the pavement-man.

At Launceston in the year that I was born
The ragged poppies ran around the corn
And red October blew her bloody gale
About the flooded field of Passchendaele.

I saw a man with sherbet in his hair
Rope camels to the coast of Russell Square
And seizing sea-coals from his burning hat
(God and the world knows what he saw in *that*!)
Print on the shaken shore with perfect hand
Poems like oak trees in a wasted land
And thresh with thunder from the sounding sky
The beating echo of a battle cry.

Then with cats, angels, saints, thugs, for the dark
Take love the last unconfidential clerk,
That flames like flowers might burn above his bed
As the white elder blossom at my head.

Now summer, and this wandering humble, hums
On the gold air epithalamiums
I and my true-love at the river's rim
These words upon the salmon-waters swim
And launch a laurel for his birthday brow—
Hoping it finds him as it leaves us now.

CHARLES CAUSLEY

The First Impact of *The Waste Land*

ROSE MACAULAY

ALL one can now do about T. S. Eliot, somewhat daunted, though illumined, by the vast library of commentary that has accrued about his works, is not to try and add to it, but to make one's personal gesture of reaction and recall, to remember the first impact on one's own mind and imagination of this poetry (for I am dealing only with the poems) as it appeared. And I chiefly remember that, beyond and through the dazzling, puzzling technique, the verbal fascination, the magpie glitter of the borrowed and adapted phrases that brought a whole chorus of literature into service, enriching and extending every theme—beyond and through all this there was the sharp sense of recognition. Here was the landscape one knew, had always known, sometimes without knowing it; here were the ruins in the soul, the shadowy dreams that lurked tenebriously in the cellars of consciousness, in the mysterious corridors and arcades of dream, the wilderness that stretches not without but within. It was not, of course, a new recognition; most imaginative poetry has shown glimpses of this waste land of the soul; the Elizabethans and Jacobeans, Dante, Shelley, Blake, Coleridge, Donne, all the great poets who had brought us up, held their torches to the ruinous and twilit world within; the human consciousness has always been recognized and explored.

Dr Browne wrote three centuries ago of 'the wonders which without further travel I can do in the cosmography of myself: there is all Africa and her prodigies in us'. All Africa, and all hell, for 'the heart of man is the place the devils dwell in; I feel sometimes a Hell within myself; Lucifer keeps his court within my breast, Legion is revived in me'. And William Law, half a century later, knew all about 'the dark fire-life of the soul'. But here now was a poet who drew from the dim corridors of the febrile and fantastic human mind, conscious and subconscious, a new wealth of associated and dis-associated images, a newly minted litter of notions, emotions, desires, fears, fantastic prodigies and dreams, the fabulous junk that gleams in the mind's cellars and on its peripheries, a shifting kaleido-scopic mosaic of images, enriched and coloured by the literature of every land and age, yet expressed in the authentic voice of one who was

> En Amérique, professeur;
> En Angleterre, journaliste . . .
> En Yorkshire, conférencier;
> A Londres, un peu banquier . . .
> En Allemagne, philosophe . . .
> J'erre toujours de-ci de-là
> A divers coups de tra là là
> De Damas jusqu'à Omàhà

and, with all his borrowings, remained himself. '*Le concert innom-brable, la grande rumeur universelle que l'on entend . . . nourrice, sans jamais l'altérer, la voix tout embrassante du poète*', which not all the overlay of French symbolists, of Ezra Pound, Dante, the Roman poets and the Greek, the Elizabethans and Jacobeans, Milton and the metaphysicals, Laforgue, the Church Fathers and the Bible, nor all the primitive legends of gods and men, could dis-guise. This seemed a new voice, revealing ancient things in a new way; the dark corridors where dreams lurk, where primeval history hides, were furnished with what seemed at times (but was not) a haphazard, inconsequent juxtaposition of images, and with frag-ments of social dialogue at tea parties, in streets, in pubs, fragments thrown up out of what mysterious context of experience? They drifted by, slipping again into the mist; their echoes disturbed.

We had been for too long used to the crude and drab simplicities of the Freudian interpretation of the subconscious mind, which tried to reduce all its manifold and intricate complexities to two roots, sex and parent-trouble; 'the beginnings of religion, ethics, society and art meet in the Oedipus complex'. We had had all that drab domestic business, the father figure and the mother-lust, and the rest of the tedious furniture of which sophisticated minds had even then grown so weary (the hold these simple theories won over minds less experienced and accurate is a measure of the naïve gullibility of the mass consciousness, so quick to accept, so slow to examine and test). Instead of all this, here was a cosmography of strange landscapes littered with the recognizable true junk of the straying imagination, the remembering mind, the deep, mindless passions below them. Here, in a limitless jungle, tracks led all ways, and eerie voices of gods, demons and strange birds called from the menacing glades, summoning lost travellers and strayed revellers on to fantastic adventures. Stars leaped and fell, owls hooted, wolves were barely kept at bay by fireworks that burst in the sky with strange whooshes, in a bright spawn of sparks. Music edged in and out; all poetry lay leaguer there, besieging, edging obliquely in, taking hold, then out again into the surrounding dark. The known landscape sprang to life: the stony waste, the decayed hole among the mountains, the empty chapel the wind's home. All this we know by nature, it is our heritage. But it is not left as we leave it; into it break thunder and voices and talk, turning the scene upside down; one has to think, to understand and follow, to look up Buddha, St Augustine, the *Upanishads*, Dante, Miss Jessie Weston and a host more of contributors to the disturbed scene. That is to say, if one does all this it is rewarding, but there is no need; the impact is made without all the reference hunting, even without all the meaning. I thought, when first I read this poetry, that the connections and sequences of thoughts and images should have been less cryptic, more obviously logical, and, well as I now know it, I think so still. But something, some elusive flavour, might have been lost in the process of clarification. Anyhow, the achieved effect of seemingly irrational emotional complexity mirrors our minds; for life is irrational and complex, the human soul is irrational and complex, the universe desperately and crazily both. No more so than it always was; our generation, our century, has no monopoly and no increase, as has sometimes been proudly claimed, of complexity, or of waste lands. T. S. Eliot's poetry is not characteristic of our age except in so far as it has largely shaped the age's poetic expression; it goes for any age. What he has done is to push out poetry's frontiers, and to turn the flickering torches of imagination rather on the inward than the outward scene, projecting it in myth, fable and phrases that sharply ironize and poeticize the tragi-comedy of man so grotesquely and sadly set in the mystery of time. What he is widely reputed to have done is to interlard his poetry with prose phrases and colloquialisms; not a new experiment, but it has gained ground immeasurably under his influence; in the hands of the unpoetic and unrhythmical it can annoy and fall flat, and is one of the complaints made against modern verse. In Mr Eliot's hands it is a delicate, piquant instrument, an elegant balance of contrasts, and puts a sharper edge on the poetry and the jargon.

One thing that was obvious from the first was that this was romantic poetry. Mr Eliot was later to say that he adhered to the classical, not the romantic, school; his verse, then and ever since, has belied him. These rigid categories are, anyhow, pretty meaningless; but, in so far as romantic has a meaning, a poetic and stylistic meaning, he is a deeply romantic poet. His poetry is a dark dream poetry, not social realism, nor calm, classically finished ordered verse. Its population, masked as merchants, socialites, prostitutes, pub-crawlers or kings and queens of legend, are ironically seen fantastics, straying befogged in a lost and alien world.

The anguished fragmentation of *The Hollow Men*, a few years after *The Waste Land*, dragged us more deeply into that desperate landscape: the surface distractions gone, only the innermost twilight kingdom, the twittering world of ghosts, was left, and a profound sense of catastrophe, heightened and deepened by a new element, fragments of the liturgy and imagery of the Christian Church, which seemed to struggle against great odds and to be defeated: this, too, one recognized as truth. Later, in *Ash-Wednesday*, preceded by the warning lights of the Ariel poems, this battle was joined again, and more intensely. Catastrophe had taken on a new dimension; continuing to exist within it, it became 'the time of tension between dying and birth'. *Ash-Wednesday* is not only a poem of great beauty, but a reaching out to a new plane of existence. To those without apprehension of this plane, it came as a deviation into an alien land, not understood or desired. By others it was understood with nostalgic recognition, and rejected. To some it presented a new and puzzling conundrum; to others it seemed a consummation of all that had preceded it, and his finest work. It brought new readers; some found here, as they had not found before, something they knew about and could grasp, even though much of its expression bewildered and seemed irrelevant. Others were converted to a quest for a religion that they had not previously intellectually esteemed; it has been said that the number of educated young people who turned towards Christianity under this influence was greater than those who, under other influences, turned towards communism, but it is doubtful if any one has actually counted. It is also true that some of his earlier readers here a little lost touch, viewing his development with some apprehension. To these, the *Four Quartets* were to come as reassurance, with their obscure and intricate technical and intellectual beauty. The setting, the closely wrought texture of interwoven verse and thought, the darting, deep-plunging imagination, the symbolism, the image and the impressive technique, combined to give confidence to the apprehensive sceptic. The Quartets are generally allowed to be Mr Eliot's finest and most finished work; the richest in content and sensibility, the most charged with thought and integrated in style.

But they are outside the range of this reminiscence, which has been seeking to recapture the memory of the first impact, to recall the excitement that perturbed and delighted us a generation ago, when that wayward brilliance broke on the poetic front. Since then a thousand or so volumes of criticism, elucidation, annotation, interpretation, discussion of influences, sources and meanings have swirled about us, explaining Mr Eliot to the world; they have saved us much trouble and research. But they do not affect this recall of a personal reaction. Nor will anything he may write in the future—and one hopes it will be much—affect this memory of excitement and recognition that opened new doors on to strange yet familiar landscapes of the moon six and thirty years ago.

'My Words Echo'

HAROLD NICOLSON

BEING two years older than T. S. Eliot, I have the right to thank him as a member of his own generation. I shall try to define the nature of the debt that I owe.

In the first place he changed, or perhaps I should say he expanded, my conception of style. Having been nurtured in the Victorian tradition, having since then become wearied by the dionysiac tunes of Swinburne, having been both attracted and repelled by Pound, Paul Fort and Apollinaire, I found in his poetry a resting-place set between the lagoons of the Nineteenth Century and the turbulent breakers which tossed and seethed outside. I was moved by the haunting cadence of his speech. I was delighted to discover that his poems, although they then seemed difficult, were, in fact, so memorable. Above all, I was impressed by the fact that, whereas his verse was liberated from the disciplines of rhyme and set metre, they retained the essential quality of song. He widened and deepened my awareness, he tuned my ear to new rhythms, he commanded attention. 'My words', he wrote in *Burnt Norton*:

> My words echo
> Thus, in your mind.

The echo still resounds.

It was not his style only that affected me. In the years after the First World War we were shattered by the futility of so much effort, the wastage of such courage, the disappointment of so many hopes. Eliot became the seer who understood and gave expression to our emptiness. Although he echoed our despair, he had small sympathy with hopelessness. He taught us that our assumptions were but 'a heap of broken images'; that the door we had never opened would remain for ever closed to us, that there was no hope of return. But he also told us that we should learn 'to care and not to care', and that as a generation we had been 'only undefeated because we had gone on trying'. He told us that we should not surrender to the agony of existence but that 'for us there is only the trying'. Although our explanations of life could never be anything more than 'hints and guesses', yet there did exist such positives as thought, discipline and action. He told us that:

> The only wisdom we can hope to acquire
> Is the wisdom of humility: humility is endless

and as an end there were faith and love. Faith which was a Grace afforded to saints only; but love which we can all achieve:

> love beyond desire, and so liberation
> From the future as well as from the past.

I do not believe that any poet less selfless and saintly than T. S. Eliot could have rescued our generation from apathy or cynicism.

Memories of T. S. E.

PHILIP MAIRET

It was in November 1934 that I first met T. S. E. in person. The occasion happened to be one of decisive importance in my working life, and this encounter made it considerably more so. Eliot had taken a lively interest in the *New English Weekly*, a periodical which had been founded two and a half years earlier by its editor A. R. Orage, and Orage had suddenly died. There was a plan for continuing this publication under my editorship, sponsored by a small committee of persons interested in the paper's survival. It was one of these, Mr W. Travers Symons, who had invited me to meet T. S. E. at his house in Woburn Square to discuss the project.

Eliot can have known hardly anything at the time of my suitability or unsuitability for the tasks of editing, which were devolving upon me simply because I had been Orage's sub-editor. Nor was I yet aware that he was strongly in favour of the existence of little periodicals such as the one we were trying to save from extinction. It was therefore a very agreeable surprise to find him ready to co-operate, even so far as to join the proposed editorial committee. Of that first conversation with him I cannot clearly recall what was said, for it was mainly about practical things and immediate circumstances; but I retain a vivid impression of his presence, and of the benevolence and sagacity he brought to bear upon the business in hand. In all that pertains to editing on the literary side he was richly experienced and I the merest beginner; but observations that I put forward with diffidence, knowing they were inadequately grounded and perhaps not very intelligent, seemed to receive his no less considerate attention. In his response they came back to me improved as if their value had appreciated by his reflection on them. I was considerably dazzled by the prospect of becoming an editor, while he, I believe, was feeling already disillusioned by the experience of it—or at least, was wearying of the labour of keeping the *Criterion* up to the high standard it maintained and of the difficulties of developing its international relations as he had hoped. But this did not at all shake his belief, expressed in his 'Last Words' to that journal when it came to an end five years afterwards, that the continuity of culture would in the future depend less upon the older organs of opinion and the commercially-viable papers, and more upon small, even obscure, organs, though they might be read by few beyond their own contributors. They were the most likely to print vital criticism and nurture writers of original talent.

It was on principle, therefore, that he was joining with us; out of pure public spirit and love of letters. Almost needless to say, his adherence not only encouraged us but went far to ensure the success of our venture—or at least its longevity, for the *New English Weekly* continued to appear for another fifteen years, which is long for a subscription journal which never had more than two thousand readers and for many years hardly a thousand.

Eliot, at forty-five, had less than the world-celebrity that accrued to his name in later years; but his standing in London literary life was unique. One like myself, who was a late entrant upon the scene, found it pervaded by his prestige, which was palpable quite beyond the circles in which one would suppose his works were read or likely to be appreciated. Even in his stronghold, Bloomsbury, one met writers who in acknowledging his importance confessed (though this was not quite the thing to do) that they were rather mystified by it. For the powerful magnetic field that was set up around this writer, whose output was so much more excellent than copious, there were reasons easier to be grasped in later perspective. In the 'twenties, that decade of disorientation, he had first charmed the *avant-garde* of writers by poetry that reflected the sense of moral and mental disarray, had then established a *Criterion* that was worthy of the name; and now, in the 'thirties, he was winning the approbation of those who cherished traditional values.

Gratified as we were by his public approval of our enterprise, we had no idea that this would be followed up by such generous participation as it was. Then and thereafter he was always better than his promises. No one looked for many occasional articles from him, but over the years his contributions to our 'Views and Reviews' feature were pretty numerous, and once or twice he even wrote some of the editorial commentary on affairs, notably some paragraphs on Mr R. A. Butler's Education Bill; but this must have been more out of friendship than inclination. He once said to me that if he had ever got into the position of having to write much and quickly he would have perished. His greatest service to the paper, beyond that of giving it articles and even poems of his own to print, was his presence among us, joining in our discussions about policy, contributors and production, generally with a kind of detachment and reserve which lent the more weight to any recommendations he offered. He was a fairly regular attendant at the fortnightly meetings of the 'Chandos Group' (so called from the name of the restaurant in which it originally met) at which, throughout the lifetime of the journal, its concerns provided the chief topics of discussion. The other most regular members of this circle were Maurice Reckitt, V. A. Demant, Geoffrey Davies, Hilderic Cousens and, later, T. M. Heron. In these clusters we had the benefit of not only T. S. E.'s wisdom but a good deal of his wit, which contrasted prettily with Reckitt's. T. S. E. once lampooned us all in clerihews, such as

Mr Philip Mairet
Crossed the Styx in a beret,
Explaining to Charon
'I must keep my hair on'

in which there may be some symbolic truth about myself which I have never fathomed. Unfortunately, the only other one of these random rhymes that I now recall is so fantastically libellous that I had better forbear to quote it. Most of T. S. E.'s lighter contributions came in the form of *mots justes* unrepeatable out of context, and our meetings were mostly too serious to provoke many of his rare and refreshing gales of laughter. After adjournment from the restaurant to Reckitt's fireside, if not before, the discussions ranged around topics seldom conducive to merriment, even apart from the recurrent crises in the journal's finances; I mean the increasingly alarming state of public affairs on which we had to form our publishable—if perishable—opinions. Taking over the conduct of the *New English Weekly* shortly after the Hitler *coup d'état*, we had to work through the period when the British public had to bear the most depressing load of anxiety in its history.

Besides these meetings with the colleagues, T. S. E. and I met pretty frequently over points of editorial and publishing business. At first these were brief—I used to drop in, or rather climb up, to his office at Fabers' on the way home to my rooms near by in Woburn Square—but as time went on we also met elsewhere for leisurely exchanges of our longer views on life and letters, causeries immensely valued by me, and of which more anon. The former were the more concerned with the practical matters in which I tried to profit by his experience; those of dealing with the younger poets and critics—a side of T. S. E.'s work of which, I suppose, I ought to know as much as anyone. For one thing, most of the best contributors to the weekly also wrote for the *Criterion*—and as a rule they wrote for it better, not only, I think, because it was a quarterly, and therefore worthy of more durable work, but because they were writing for Eliot.

I think a good part of T. S. E.'s best influence on the younger intelligentsia was communicated personally through his ministrations as editor and publisher; not, of course, that that would have been possible but for the importance of his own work. No poet and critic of his calibre, so far as I know, has been also a publisher, and this has brought him into personal contact with many more of the aspirants to a literary life than he would otherwise have met or corresponded with. He treated them all, including the less promising, as fellow-artists in the craft, while they looked up to him as a master who might also help them to publication. He is not a personal teacher by nature—as, for instance, I take Ezra Pound to have been, especially in the days of Eliot's earlier intimacy with him. To instruct many others about their work by having to pronounce judgment on it is a function that devolved on T. S. E. by circumstances and was discharged by him, one feels, often at an expense of spirit and even against the grain. My impression is that his literary clients were seldom treated to much direct explanation, analysis or exhortation;

in no role is Eliot what you would call expansive; but he had always studied work submitted to him with generous attention, and his reactions, positive or negative, had no less weight for being usually brief. One felt there was more behind them; and that his decisions were motivated by pure intellectual justice, pronounced with great caution, but with a clarity likely to get right home. Another thing to which I attach more importance than I can briefly explain is that Eliot was not different from what his writing had led you to expect. This is by no means always so; again I recall, for instance, Pound, whose amiable and gentle presence was apt to surprise devotees who had known him only by his poetry, his criticism—or his personal letters. Indeed, I once entertained a theory that many of the people who take to letters do so in the exercise of a side of their personality that life has prevented them from expressing; an idea that would not at all apply to Eliot and his works.

Although, in trying to make the *New English Weekly* a seed-plot for new writers, I had the benefit of T. S. E.'s example and advice, he was in no way responsible for my conduct of this part of our policy, least of all for my numerous errors and misjudgments. Our fostering of new talents may have produced less than that of Orage when he ran *The New Age* for just the same number of years, beginning in 1907. But conditions were then more propitious. Of writers who found their first, or almost their first, platform with us in the 1930's and '40s, George Orwell and Dylan Thomas became famous, and a fair number of others became successful writers or producers for broadcasting. They all helped to attract attention to the paper as a free forum of intelligent minority opinion, one to which established writers also, such as Herbert Read, Bonamy Dobrée, Edwin Muir and Denis Saurat, contributed both on principle and whenever they wanted to write something unlikely to be printed elsewhere. For the first four or five years most of the Editorial Notes were written by Albert Newsome, who brilliantly developed the line of economic and financial criticism initiated by the previous editor Orage, but the emphasis gradually shifted from this towards longer perspectives and a more philosophic criticism of current trends. We discussed the prospects of world-technical civilization, not only from the standpoint of present politics but of resources both human and natural, well before those topics attained to the headline status they have now—and even now few realize their ever-growing importance in a world that is committed without limit to technics, equalitarianism and raising the material standards of living. It was in my thinking about the conservation of values under these conditions that I made the closest contact with Eliot's mind, and he, I believe, with mine.

It was this subject, which is really that of the philosophy of culture, that we were chiefly concerned with at our less frequent, longer meetings for quiet conversation. Our preoccupation with it started, I fancy, one memorable night when we had groped our way through the black-out from our usual restaurant in the Euston Road to my fireside in Bloomsbury; where we discussed the cultural influence of Goethe, with whom he was just beginning to make the effort to reconcile himself. Eliot had just finished writing his *The Idea of a Christian Society*, which from one point of view is an essay in the philosophy of culture; and a little later in the war we tried together to run a series of conversational classes on the nature of culture at St Anne's House in Soho, when it was opened as a 'House of Christian discourse'. The best result of this experiment in which I seconded him was that it started him on the writing of his *Notes towards the Definition of Culture*, published in 1948.

The war years were those in which I saw most of him, partly because we were both on the Board of Dr J. H. Oldham's *Christian News-Letter* from its beginning in 1939. When its meetings were held at a house in Belgrave Square, we sometimes walked back from them to Victoria and stopped for needed refreshment at the station buffet or in a milk bar, where we conversed through the buzz of voices and the clatter of tea-tackle. Memory seems to recall brief moments of rare philosophic serenity in these uncomfortable colloquies, though they were chiefly ruminations on the apprehensions and worries of that interval of 'phoney' war. Eliot had just issued his last *Criterion*, in a depression of spirits about public affairs which he said was 'so different from any other experience of fifty years as to be a new emotion'. Yet something he said to me here, in reply to an unconsidered expression of mine about patriotism, gave me a sudden realization that he, while fully sharing the emotional involvement in the political situation, did so with a detachment of spirit I could not maintain, so that his response pierced me like a rebuke. This was not the only time that he convicted me, without personal intention on his part, of a judgment distorted by passion, a quality in which I had rather thought myself deficient. In politics and culture Eliot almost holds with Acton, that 'our studies ought to be pursued with chastity, like mathematics'.

I allude to this incident only because I fancy it is representative of Eliot's personal effects on others to whom he has communicated a moment of truth, not didactically but by being who he is. The essential Eliot, who is explicit only in his later poems, remains above our talking with him—mine, at any rate, though we have gone into some lofty questions. But at some moment, as it were through a rift in the discussion, you may get a glimpse of the mind you had encountered in reading the poetry. Or the glimpse may come in his absence, attached not to a quotation but to an uncalled-for recollection of himself, which is in some way relevant to a critical turn in what one is thinking or doing. At least, I have known this happen to me, with decisive effects, and I should think it must have occurred to others in his wide circle of friends.

On one of the evenings that finished in the milk bar, T. S. E. made me the finest present that any editor ever received from a poet—the second of the *Four Quartets*. Of these the first had appeared already elsewhere: the third and fourth he also presented to the *New English Weekly* as they came from his pen. Eliot's princely largesse to voluntary journalism as a cultural cause—which looks more and more like being a lost cause—did not save our little weekly from extinction when the time came; but his persistence in that cause has continued, as we saw, for instance, when he gave an important essay on the writing of dramatic poetry to *Adam*, the little review produced by Mr Miron Grindea. I fear this interest of Eliot's may not appeal to many, because it is not so easy to see the beauty of intellectual charity as of other kinds of charity, or to realize its irreplaceable importance if the springs of culture are not to dry up.

This relates also to T. S. E.'s work in the publishing of books, in which department also I have had the privilege of a good deal of co-operation with him. Of the costly attention he has devoted to new or obscure authors I could a tale unfold; I mean, of his care that work in which he discerned value should not perish, though it might be quite unpublishable without onerous revision. Many people must have thought that the trouble he took in this direction was a work of supererogation, or even regrettable in a creative writer already heavily occupied in other ways; but I am sure he did not think so. The altogether rare kind of responsibility that he brought to publishing meant more than nursing the offspring of writers who are better thinkers than writers—though this can involve one in labours and in decisions that are harassing enough. A higher spiritual expense is liable to be incurred in deciding whether to sponsor the work of authors who may have undeniable competence of some kind, and are venturing into yet uncharted oceans of thought, such as those that separate the cultural and religious continents of the West from those of the East. The same is true of works that seriously challenge the 'collective representations' of this age of science. It may not be possible to do justice here without entering into the speculative discourse of other minds to a very considerable extent, trying to make connections with one's own intellectual perspective, and being drawn into realms of thought one cannot participate. This is no light matter for anyone, and must be especially wearing to a creative mind with its own well-developed way of thinking. Whether T. S. E. could say with Goethe 'I have been clever, my lad, I never thought about thinking', I do not presume to know. But even if he could, the detached entertainment of alien philosophic views must have put additional strain upon the energies devoted to this side of his work.

All this, however, is part and parcel of the burden he was destined by nature and training to assume—that of vindicating criteria in a period of extraordinary cultural confusion. I would emphasize the range of his mind and the scope of his activities because they have received much less recognition than the originality of his poetry. It may be that only his poetry will very long survive; but the poetry elucidates the same values that he has been concerned to defend in other spheres, notably in that of international literature and learning, where his activity has been imperfectly appreciated owing to the insular climate of opinion in his adopted country. Firmly re-rooted as he is in England, Eliot is great as a European man of letters, and one who is highly conscious of the crisis in world culture which European Christendom has brought about. I should not know where to look for finer statements about the European heritage, its nature and its present and prospective importance, than his recent lectures delivered in Germany. I am thinking of those on 'The Unity of European Culture', and the magnificent lecture on Goethe.

In finishing an article like this, for a commemorative volume, one is sensitive of being thought to have dwelt monotonously on the note of appreciation. Doubtless if I had any skill in literary portraiture I should have tried to make artful use of such instances as I could recall, of my subject's misjudgments, or his inabilities to cope with particular situations—things incidental to any man thoroughly committed to a job of work in the world—if only to paint in a few shadows and set off the high-lights of the picture to better effect. But the purpose with which I began these notes was only to recall my own impressions of him, chiefly at work, over a period of more than twenty years of friendship, and of intermittent collaboration in activities outside those which have made him famous. I have been recollecting, chiefly, what I have seen of his relations with other persons and groups of persons, but I have been conscious all the time of his own poetic and critical work as I understand it. And what emerges from these septuagenarian ruminations is that I find I cannot think of him as a friendly presence and a man of affairs quite apart from what he is as a poet. It seems to me that the same wisdom that is in the poetry was concealed in these relatively obscure activities where he was dealing, actively or passively, with other persons and their works.

'O City City'

PAUL JENNINGS

WHEN I first read, years ago, that Mr Eliot had worked in a bank, my first impulse was to find out which bank, and which branch, and to join it. Even if this should mean cashing my cheques in Tulse Hill or, more likely, somewhere in the city

> Where fishmen lounge at noon: where the walls
> Of Magnus Martyr hold
> Inexplicable splendour of Ionian white and gold

(*what* a line!), it would be worth it, to get so close to the marvellous paradox of a poet in a bank. Particularly Mr Eliot in a bank.

I did not hope specifically that I should meet some actual manager or cashier who would say 'Ah, yes, I remember Mr Eliot. He and I were young fellers together in the mortgage department, under Mr Batty (Sir Hector Batty, he is now). Funny thing, we all called him *Mr* Eliot, even Mr Batty did. Dry chap, he was. Bit of a poet, too, always talking to the office cat. I remember once Mr Batty sent him out to get a surveyor's report on some property for a client; old house had been a dancing school. Most of us young chaps used to like a job like that, meant an afternoon out of the office, you know. But not Mr Eliot. He seemed to like just sitting there, thinking. This time, he came back, I can see him now, just stood in the doorway and said *The houses are all gone under the sea. The dancers are all gone under the hill.* Couldn't get a word out of him the whole afternoon. Of course, he didn't stay with us long. I heard he had something to do with the theatre afterwards.'

No, nothing so simple as that, although it would have been fun. The paradox is much deeper than the mere opposition of banker and poet. It is the paradox of every true Artist As A Young Man, living in temporary and deceptive harmony with the world as he finds it before he changes it; looking just like other men, doing the humdrum jobs that they do, while all the time strange fires are building up inside him, he is the crucible of a monstrous change. Indeed, there is an even sharper paradox in Mr Eliot; for his poignant discovery, in the middle of a world made by bankers and industrialists, of what Chesterton called The Thing—Western, traditional, Christian civilization—affected English poetry in a far more revolutionary manner than did the wildest experiments of what one might call professional revolutionaries.

On the back of the dust-jacket of almost any novel nowadays one may read of the fantastic career of the author, who before he is twenty-five has been a dishwasher in Paris, a lion-tamer, a prospector, a lighthouse-keeper, a tramp, a medical student, secretary to a Greek millionaire, and even a salesman in a Leicester furniture shop. This is all very well in its way and doubtless provides experience. But a bank would not provide 'experience' in this way for Mr Eliot. He is not the sort of poet who can be found in that anthology with which all readers of this book, being civilized persons, will doubtless be familiar—*The Stuffed Owl*, Mr D. B. Wyndham Lewis's famous collection of bad verse. There are plenty of poems about direct banking experience *there*. Here, for instance, is the Earl of Lytton, in *Lucile*:

> A fortnight ago a report about town
> Made me most apprehensive. Alas and alas!
> I at once wrote and warn'd you. Well, now let that pass.
> A run on the Bank about five days ago
> Confirmed my forebodings too terribly, though
> I drove to the City at once—
>
> *etcetera.*

Or even a reputable poet like Crabbe:

> Something one day occurr'd about a bill
> That was not drawn with true mercantile skill
> And I was asked and authorised to go
> To seek the firm of Clutterbuck and Co.

Your true poet does not tie up little desiccated parcels of reality in this fashion. He is concerned with essences, or rather with the flickering human spark that jumps between the gap of the real and the unreal. The true significance of Mr Eliot's banking (as a matter of fact it was Lloyds Bank, and he dealt not with mortgages but with 'documentary bills, acceptances', whatever those are, 'and foreign exchange') is that it brought him immediately to the heart of contemporary reality—

History is now and England

the reality of a world whose motive power is the strange dead dynamism of commerce. Lewis Mumford, speaking of the 'analytical decomposition of the church', says:

> The nave, the bare assembly place, became the bourse. Do not imagine that [this] is a wild imaginary parallel: in the seventeenth century the brokers plied their trade in the nave of St Paul's, and the money-changers all but drove the representatives of Christ from the temple—till at last the stench became too great for even a venal church to endure. Wren's unused plan for the reconstruction of London after the fire handsomely recognized this new order of life. He did not give the dominating site to St Paul's: he planned the new avenues to give this honour to the Stock Exchange.

Anyone who has ever been in a bank must at some time have had the feeling that he is at the gross, physical end, rather like the Hindu *bhutas*, of a huge system—rather, come to think of it, like Hinduism—in which there are ascending orders of reality, subtler and subtler resolutions of opposites, until the absolute Brahma is reached. All that sordid business with cheques and shovelfuls of pennies and the rest of it is the lowest form of the bank's activity. Behind those glass doors, those solid mahogany partitions, things get more profound. They shut the doors at 3, they start a kind of financial yoga, they meditate on money and not-money. Wise, old, disillusioned men contemplate the flickering dance of money across the world. *Money was over-plentiful in the discount market yesterday. The dollar cross-rate rose sharply. Transferable pounds in Zürich eased from* $2.7550.60 to $2.7730.40. These men know that Zürich, the lake, the bright clean Swiss in their trim grey trains, are one reality, London is another, both are real and unreal:

What is that city over the mountains
Cracks and reforms and bursts in the violet air
Falling towers
Jerusalem Athens Alexandria
Vienna London
Unreal.

Right at the centre of the banking world are heavy-lidded old men, dead and burningly alive, who survey all things with the terrible clarity of Dostoievsky's Grand Inquisitor.

Mr Eliot, on documentary bills, acceptances and foreign exchange, evidently got some way in this hierarchy. But he was not destined to become a *saddhu*. To some eyes his glory is less, to others more: but he became instead a poet, speaking to us earthbound ones in other accents, other idioms, showing us other aspects of reality. Who can fail to be excited at the thought of the marvellous symbols of contradiction—the intersection of time and timeless, the winter sunshine, the unimaginable zero summer—being slowly fertilized in Mr Eliot's mind by this dialectic of banks? Moving in the dreamy routine of the bank, he would glimpse outside the windows tall red buses, people, birds, fragments of the real; and into the gloomy office, on fearful wings, would sweep desperate, beautiful images of escape and ecstasy with the One:

From the wide window towards the granite shore
The white sails still fly seaward, seaward fly
Unbroken wings.

Lloyds' loss is our gain.

Lewis Carroll and T. S. Eliot as Nonsense Poets

ELIZABETH SEWELL

'He thought he saw a Banker's Clerk
  Descending from a bus:
He looked again, and found it was
  A Hippopotamus.'

'I saw the 'potamus take wing.'

IT WAS Chesterton, that man of marvellous perception and often perverse practice, who announced in 1904 that Nonsense was the literature of the future. It was a brilliant guess. Even now, however, when it is clear that he was right, when the trials in Wonderland and the Snark have become prototypes of real trials from Reichstag to McCarthy, and much of our literature—poetry and criticism—and most of our philosophy is shaped on Nonsense principles, people are slow to recognize its importance, or that of Lewis Carroll. Carroll is no *lusus naturae* but a central figure, as important for England, and in the same way, as Mallarmé is for France. Nonsense is how the English choose to take their Pure Poetry, their *langage mathématique* or *romances sans paroles*: their struggle to convert language into symbolic logic or music. It is a serious struggle, but taken this way it need not appear so. Nonsense? A mere game, of course. This is characteristic of us. We like, you might say, to play possum in these matters.

The genre or game of Nonsense has strict rules. The aim is to construct with words a logical universe of discourse meticulously selected and controlled; within this playground the mind can then manipulate its material, consisting largely of names of things and numbers. The process is directed always towards analysing and separating the material into a collection of discreet counters, with which the detached intellect can make, observe and enjoy a series of abstract, detailed, artificial patterns of words and images (you may be reminded of the New Criticism), which have their own significance in themselves. All tendencies towards synthesis are taboo: in the mind, imagination and dream; in language, the poetic and metaphorical elements; in subject-matter, everything to do with beauty, fertility and all forms of love, sacred or profane. Whatever is unitive is the great enemy of Nonsense, to be excluded at all costs.

The pure practice of Nonsense demands a high degree of asceticism, since its very existence in the mind depends on limitation and infertility. Nonsense is by nature logical and anti-poetic. The Nonsense poet, therefore, faces a constant paradox of self-denial. Something of the effects of this can be seen in the work of three great Nonsense practitioners, Mallarmé, Carroll and Mr T. S. Eliot.

Mallarmé devoted his life, at great cost, to this paradox, becoming in the course of it an ascetic, atheistic, secular saint of letters. Neither Carroll nor Mr Eliot was content to do this, and in their attitude and literary production they can be seen to resemble one another, their progressions describing similar curves, perhaps characteristic of great Nonsense men: they begin with strict Nonsense of a high order, but then, chafing at the game's restrictions, they desire to include some or all of those elements of real life—human relationships, the body, sex, love, religion, growth and development in the natural world—which Nonsense rules out. The desire is noble but it disintegrates the game. Mallarmé in the end cunningly escapes the paradox by progressing to thinking about thinking, in *Un Coup de Dés*, allowing himself a dangerously beautiful if shadowy ship and ocean and a sudden miraculous precipitation of stars, yet keeping the overall figure of dice-play, which is numbers and a game, and so could be Nonsense still. The Eliot-Mallarmé connection is close, Mr Eliot himself providing clues to it in 'Lines for an Old Man' and *Little Gidding*; but the Eliot-Carroll connection is closer. With Carroll we move from pure Nonsense in the *Alices* through *The Hunting of the Snark* to *Sylvie and Bruno*, and with Mr Eliot from *The Waste Land* and the poems of the Sweeney period through the *Four Quartets* to the late plays. Carroll is the best interpreter we have for Mr Eliot, and *Old Possum's Book of Practical Cats,* Mr Eliot's overt Nonsense work, is not a chance production, the master in a lighter mood. It is integral to the whole body of his work, and a key to his poetry and his problem.

Mr Eliot couches his own autobiography in Nonsense terms, but at one remove, for he parodies Lear's *Autobiography* into 'How unpleasant to meet Mr Eliot!' He is an extensive parodist as Carroll was, and in each case this is a device for handling what might otherwise be dangerous for Nonsense. It is a matter of affirming and denying, and in his autobiography Mr Eliot affirms and denies Nonsense in its relation to himself. He has told us that he drew from *Alice in Wonderland* that rose-garden with which the first of the *Four Quartets* opens, leading into the image of the rose which pervades and closes the last of them. In his 1929 essay on the Dante he so greatly reveres he says that we have 'to pass through the looking-glass into a world which is just as reasonable as our own. When we have done that we begin to wonder whether the world of Dante is not both larger and more solid than our own'. Nonsense goes deep in Mr Eliot. One does not describe one's life, even ironically, construct an image system in serious poetry, nor interpret an honoured poet in terms of something one considers trivial. It is we who would be at fault in seeing Nonsense so. What Mr Eliot is doing here is working at the dilemma of his vocation as a Nonsense poet. The *Four Quartets* epitomize the problem. They are religious poems; yet one of their main images comes from classical Nonsense, the Wonderland rose which becomes the *Paradiso* rose drawn in its turn from a poet to understand whom, according to Mr Eliot, we have to go through the looking-glass. And Nonsense as a pure systematic art-form of mind and language excludes both poetry and religion.

Lewis Carroll, much less of a poet than Mr Eliot but no less devoted a churchman, faces the same problem. He had, however, two advantages: first, he had an official status in the matter; second, he was luckier in his period. He had a triple identity, as the Reverend Charles Dodgson, as a professional mathematician and symbolic logician, and as a Nonsense writer. The last two, closely allied as they are, were allowed to meet; the first was sealed off, at least up till the *Sylvie and Bruno* period. And the age in which he lived, a pre-Freudian era in which more modern meanings of 'repressions' or 'integration' were unknown, made possible such a separation and that which resulted from it—the perfection of the *Alices.* (The *Snark* is already much more ambiguous.) It is a pattern that Mr Eliot might almost envy, if only for its true Nonsense quality. He, in his Nonsense autobiography, describes his own features as being 'of clerical cut',[1] and it is remarkable how character after character in the plays is impelled towards Holy Orders. Harry in *Family Reunion* departs for 'a stony sanctuary and a primitive altar'; Celia in *The Cocktail Party* joins an order, 'a very austere one', and is martyred; Eggerson in *The Confidential Clerk* announces that Colby Simpkins will soon be entering the Church; and in *Murder in the Cathedral* the protagonist is archbishop, saint and martyr already. Mr Eliot's difficulty is that nowadays religion and other such vital subjects cannot conveniently be affirmed and then closed off. One has to be Nonsense man, poet and churchman all at once. Carroll's hippopotamus, secure in its Nonsense bounds, can remain of the earth, earthy; but Mr Eliot's has got into the poetry and has somehow to be got into heaven. Yet despite the superficial differences between them, to us readers it is a great help to have one such quadruped by which to measure a second, and Carroll is the best point of reference we have for understanding Mr Eliot.

Anyone interested in drawing minor parallels between earlier Eliot poems and the *Alices* will find material ready to hand: the reminiscence of the Frog Footman in *Portrait of a Lady* ('I shall sit here . . .'); the executioner who haunts *Sweeney Agonistes* among the playing-cards as he does the Queen's croquet game; the echo, also in *Sweeney*, of the riddle of the Red King's dream, 'If he was alive then the milkman wasn't'; the reversals or full-stops of time in the two writers; the endless tea-party, interminable as the Hatter's, in *Prufrock*, *Portrait of a Lady*, 'Mr Apollinax', 'Hysteria', 'A Cooking Egg', *The Waste Land* where the typist comes home at tea-time, the

[1] Ezra Pound in the Cantos refers to Mr Eliot as either 'the Rev. Eliot' or 'Old Possum', as if he, too, saw the dilemma of the connection.

first scene of *Family Reunion*, Skimbleshanks in *Old Possum*, till only the tea-leaves are left in *The Dry Salvages*; and so on. These are not uninteresting, but they are very minor affairs. It is in the major poems, as it should be, that Carroll and Nonsense begin to be really helpful.

The Waste Land is comparable to the *Alices* and to them alone, as Mr Eliot's nearest approach to pure Nonsense practice. He admits certain elements into his subject-matter—myth, love, the poetry and beauty of the past—which are dangerous, but he employs classic Nonsense techniques to control them. Thus the fragmentation in the poem is not to be regarded, in this light, as a lament on our modern condition. It is the Nonsense poet's way of analysing his subject-matter into discrete parts, 'one and one and one' as the Red Queen says,[1] to make it workable in Nonsense terms. The same is true of the sterility the poem deals with. This, too, is the Nonsense poet carefully setting up the conditions necessary for the exercise of his special art. To hold the whole poem together, the two classic Carroll frameworks are employed, playing-cards and chess, the digits and moves of a game substituted for those dangerous and un-Nonsense entities, human relationships. The Nonsense rules procure the necessary working conditions—detachment of mind from subject-matter, analysis of material, manipulation of patterns of unfused images. Into this careful systematics, highly intellectual as Nonsense is, even potentially subversive material can be fitted and held, and the result is probably Mr Eliot's masterpiece.

With the *Four Quartets*, the situation is made more difficult by what is now the poet's increasing emphasis upon unitive subjects, particularly love and religion. We need here, as points of reference, the *Alices* and the *Snark*, with a glance forward to *Sylvie and Bruno*. The overall Nonsense control of *The Waste Land* has gone; in its place we have Nonsense procedures still operating, but used now as defences against particular dangers. We will consider four of these: poetry, words in their non-logical functions, and the two central images, roses and dancing.

Traditional forms of poetry are admitted into the Quartets from

[1] For the end of the poem particularly, the Baker in *The Hunting of the Snark* is also a helpful commentator: 'I said it in Hebrew, I said it in Dutch, / I said it in German and Greek', etc.

time to time, with their complement of metaphor and non-logical speech so antithetical to Nonsense. When they appear, however, they tend, as in the *Alices*, to be pounced on and immediately subjected to critical analysis. See Part II of *East Coker*, for instance, where the passage 'What is the late November doing' is followed at once by

> That was a way of putting it—not very satisfactory.
> A periphrastic study in a worn-out poetical fashion.

So Alice says to the Caterpillar after repeating some verses, 'Not quite right, I'm afraid. . . . Some of the words have got altered', and receives the reply, 'It is wrong from beginning to end'. Poetry is dangerous to Nonsense, even if unsatisfactory, even if parodied, and it is as well to reduce it to criticism at once. No one interested in the present hypertrophied condition of literary criticism should overlook the importance of the Caterpillar and Humpty Dumpty as spiritual ancestors of this development.

Words, the materials of poetry with their aura of figures and dreams, are perilous, too. Mr Eliot's description of his own conversation, restricted so nicely to What Precisely, acknowledges the Nonsense rule: words must be rigorously controlled lest dream and poetry creep in. So *Burnt Norton* says that words decay with imprecision, will not stay in place, will not stay still, to which Humpty Dumpty adds, 'They've a temper, some of them, particularly verbs'. In *East Coker* comes the phrase 'the intolerable wrestle with words and meanings', and the complaint that one has only learnt to get the better of words for the thing that one no longer has to say; but the obligation is to master the words, as Humpty confirms, 'The question is, which is to be master, that's all'. A poet may be in part at least subject to his words; a Nonsense poet never. Only at the end of *Little Gidding* are the words allowed out to dance, and even then they have to be formal, exact, precise. So we come to dancing and roses, the two great Dante images for heaven which are also Nonsense images in Carroll and Eliot poetry.

A rose is about as dangerous an image for Nonsense as could be imagined. It implies an immense range of living company—beauty, growth, the body, sex, love. Roses in Nonsense will need special treatment, and Carroll begins to operate on his immediately, with pots of paint wielded by playing-card people or animated numbers. Mr Eliot adopts a different but no less effective technique, sterilizing his rose in his turn, at the beginning and end of *Little Gidding*, with ice and fire which cancel one another out and wipe away with them the living notion of the rose, leaving only a counter or cipher, suitable for Nonsense, behind.

Lastly, there is the dance, a dangerously living and bodily image, too. Carroll's attitude to it is always insecure. The cavorting Mock Turtle and Gryphon are clumsy and tread on Alice's feet; three times round the mulberry bush is enough for Tweedledum and Tweedledee. Carroll's most revealing dance occurs in one of his letters, where he compares his own dancing to a rhinoceros and hippopotamus executing a minuet together. Carroll is the reluctant dancing hippo. Mr Eliot is a reluctant dancer also in the Quartets, even though dancing is the way to heaven. The dance is constrained: 'At the still point, there the dance is', restricted as the circling round the Mad Hatter's table or the crocodile walking up his own forehead in *Sylvie and Bruno*. The best comment on this inhibition of free movement comes in the *Snark*. 'In my beginning is my end or say that the end precedes the beginning', it runs in *East Coker* and *Burnt Norton*, and the Bellman, familiar with this condition, describes it as being 'snarked', a state when 'the bowsprit got mixed with the rudder sometimes'. Movement in Nonsense is admitted only to be annulled, if the control and pattern are to be preserved.

Where then can we go now? It seems only towards *Sylvie and Bruno*, *The Cocktail Party*, *The Confidential Clerk*. There is already a surprising similarity between Part II of *The Dry Salvages*,

> Where is there an end of it, the soundless wailing,
> The silent withering of autumn flowers

and so on, and the prose-poem with which *Sylvie and Bruno* ends, with its chilly mists and wailing gusts over the ocean, its withered leaves of a blighted hope, and the injunction, to the hero sailing for India, 'Look Eastward!' as the Eliot poem bears us on to Krishna and Arjuna. Yet this is not Mr Eliot's last word as Nonsense poet.

He will talk about love and God and heaven in the later Quartets and plays, as Carroll does in *Sylvie and Bruno Concluded*, but this is not the answer, nor the way in which the hippopotamus can enter heaven. Mr Eliot's answer is more direct and much more surprising; one hesitates, with any writer calling his book *Old Possum*, to suggest that it seems also largely unconscious. He implies that the way for a Nonsense poet to reach heaven is by Nonsense itself; and so we have *Old Possum's Book of Practical Cats*.

Cats and Nonsense writers agree well together, in life and in books. Cats are images for the body and for woman (so Grishkin) but in appeasable form. It is possible that cats are also images for God, in miniature. Mr Empson suggests that the Cheshire Cat represented God, and I believe that the GREAT RUMPUSCAT (Mr Eliot's capitals) might do so, too. *Gerontion*, after all, speaks openly of Christ the tiger. But here there is no menace, Mr Eliot can permit himself liberties Carroll never took, and sly theological eddies wander through the Possum book, in 'Old Deuteronomy', or the cat's three names, one of which is ineffable. In this so-called minor work can be found all the love and charity which cause Mr Eliot, as Nonsense poet, so much trouble in the rest of his poetry, but released and reconciled. Here, too, sin is behovely ('I could mention Mungojerrie, I could mention Griddlebone') but all shall be well; and there is set moving in 'The Song of the Jellicles', at long last and in despite of all impediments and far beyond any of the supposedly more poetic works, a dance so free and loving and joyful, yet quiet and half-secret, that it is a clear image of heaven, and an invitation thither.

Since there is in any case a ball in preparation here, and it seems the merest accident that Mr Eliot left one thing out of this his most beautiful Nonsense poem, may I make the omission good, and offer, in recognition and gratitude, a rose for the Jellicles.

From *The Rock* to *The Confidential Clerk*

E. MARTIN BROWNE

THIS essay covers only five dramatic works. It is a shock to realize this, when one is aware of the range of possibilities that Mr Eliot has opened out for a producer. No other dramatist can have made so great an impact on the theatre with so small an output. It has been my privilege to produce all five of his full-length works for the first time, and the reflections that follow arise from that series of experiences.

I have not used the word 'play' in description of the five, because the first, *The Rock*, was not a play. The conception was not Mr Eliot's own—nor indeed was it mine, though the scenario on which he ultimately worked was devised by me. A pageant was called for, to promote the building of churches in Greater London. In the middle 'thirties opportunities for a poet to write for the theatre were almost non-existent, and Mr Eliot was tempted by this one, as well as sympathetic to the cause. After many months in which we found ourselves equally puzzled by the problem of how to create an interesting form while retaining the pageant-elements demanded, we agreed on a scenario based on the structure of the type of revue then current under the aegis of Charles Cochran: the difference being that instead of the Young Ladies relying on their physical charms, they (together with their male counterparts) wore half-masks and garments of stiff hessian and relied on the application of their vocal agility to Mr Eliot's verse. He created for them a series of Choruses which contain some of his finest dramatic poetry, and was rewarded by hearing large audiences at Sadler's Wells receive its humour with delight and its lyricism with exaltation.

The producer's problem with regard to this verse was a simple one, for the speakers were impersonal beings whose only function was to make those comments which the author had set down for them, and accordingly the only requirement was a suitable and pleasing grouping during the delivery of the lines. The action of the work was not in the hands of the Chorus, and therefore does not directly bear upon the study I am undertaking in this essay.

The success of *The Rock* caused the Friends of Canterbury Cathedral to invite Mr Eliot to write the first new play for their annual festival, in 1935. This event also fell right outside the orbit of the theatre as it then existed: the run envisaged was eight performances in a medieval hall of great discomfort, seating less than five hundred people, and the cast would, for financial and local reasons, be at least partly amateur. Yet, once more, Mr Eliot accepted. The play he wrote was *Murder in the Cathedral.*

The conditions of the original production are not worth recording, except in so far as they influenced the writer. The Chapter House is a rectangular building ninety feet long, and in those days had no exit except the one door at the back of the auditorium, leading into the Cloisters. The platform constructed for the play had to be shallow to allow as much room as possible for the audience; at the back were *sedilia* used by the monastic dignitaries at Chapter meetings. There was, of course, no front curtain and no scenery. The body of the murdered Archbishop Becket lay upon the stage until the end of the play, when it was carried in procession down the central aisle and round the Cloisters to the singing of the Litany of the Saints, introduced by the last words of the Chorus.

These conditions, studied by Mr Eliot, inclined him to a construction analogous in certain respects to the medieval, notably in the use of liturgical forms (*Dies Irae*, *Te Deum*) and the introduction of the Sermon, as well as in the type of verse used in the dialogue scenes. But added to these products of the place was a Chorus on the Greek model which played a dominant part in the structure and had assigned to it most of the finest poetry in the play.

This Chorus provides one of the most challenging problems in contemporary drama for the producer, especially when, as happened a year or two later, the play is transferred from the special setting for which it was written and has to adapt itself to a Victorian type of theatre-building. The Chorus is often dismissed as theatrically an outmoded survival, however fine its language may be: but this is in my view a grave misjudgment. True, the play is in form the closest of all Mr Eliot's plays to the Classic Greek (and in one way or another that has been his source of inspiration as a dramatist throughout). The Chorus speaks formal odes between scenes; it is deprived, as the Greek Chorus was, of the right to participate in the action. But it is not as impersonal as even Euripides's Choruses: and Mr Eliot clearly does not see it dancing; he thinks of its members, in fact, more as *dramatis personae*, more as a group of individuals gripped by common emotions. This is in line with his Christian approach; and owes something also to the influence of the modern drama with its concentration upon the individual.

How then is it to be treated in production? In the original showing the treatment was conditioned by an ecclesiastical building decorated with Victorian-Gothic painting, against which the Chorus had to be seen for the entire play and from which they must stand out. This suggested, first, a high degree of formality; secondly, a colour scheme brilliant enough to have the effect of stained glass. When (first of all for economic reasons) this was carried over into the theatre, it seemed to me progressively more unsatisfactory; I believe that the treatment which was given at the Old Vic in 1953 was nearer to thc right one. This used a colour scheme which suggested both the drab clothes of the poor and sculptured stone, and thus allowed both for the realism of

> We have brewed beer and cyder
> Talked at the corners of streets
> Talked not always in whispers

and for the classicism of

> Dead upon the tree, my Saviour,
> Let not be in vain thy labour
> Help me, Lord, in my last fear

and bound both together in the passionate immobilities of appeal:

The Lords of Hell are here.
They curl round you, lie at your feet, swing and wing through the dark air.
O Thomas Archbishop, save us, save us, save yourself that we may be saved.
Destroy yourself and we are destroyed.

But the Chorus depends upon the speaking and acting quite as much as on the dressing. Choral speaking has in its modern revival suffered much from the excessive individualism of the theatre (holding the mirror up to an excessively individualistic age), and is always entered upon by actors with an acute self-consciousness, whether of enthusiasm or of fear. To be successful, the Chorus of *Murder in the Cathedral* ought to be composed of women of widely differing ages, from one or two adolescents to women as old as can compass the extremely difficult task of learning lines in a Chorus (far harder than when all your cues come from individuals and all your lines are yours alone). This means that to make it work really well one must have a biggish group of women, all of whom are willing to be members of a group, yet all of whom have some marked individual quality. The only time I have ever satisfied myself in this respect was in my last production in Gloucester Cathedral (July 1955) with a Chorus of sixteen. In the theatre earlier I had been progressively reducing the numbers I used, and it is probably not wise to use so many on an enclosed stage as in an open arena such as the Cathedral provided.

The speaking of this Chorus has to cover the whole range from the moment of individual experience:

The young man mutilated,
The torn girl trembling by the millstream

to the ritual universality of praise:

We praise Thee, O God, for Thy Glory displayed in all the creatures of the earth,
In the snow, in the rain, in the wind, in the storm, in all of Thy creatures, both the hunters and the hunted.

It has also, technically, to be capable of a great variety of rhythm and of taking very long phrases in a single sweep. Emotionally, it has to be totally free from self-pity (the ultimate sin in acting) and free also from the *sound* of self-pity, which is often due not to an emotional state but to a lack of tonal control. It has to ring true as individual experience, and to carry conviction (not the sanctimonious substitute) in its declarations of faith. It has to communicate with the audience effectively enough to win its participation in the final acknowledgement

> That the sin of the world is upon our heads; that the blood of the martyrs and the agony of the saints
> Is upon our heads.

I have devoted so much space to the Chorus because it is the most important single factor in the success of the play from the author's point of view, and the most difficult. The other question most discussed is that of the Knights' apology. Should they be played by the same actors as the Tempters, in order to underline the continuity of the assault upon Becket? Mr Eliot now prefers that they should not. Originally, the plan had advantages (besides the economic) in defining the nature of the shock delivered by the First Knight's famous opening: 'We beg you to give us your attention for a few moments.'

It is hard to remember now how great this shock was in 1935, when poetic drama was something holily and completely separate from drama. There was a danger, hard to combat, that the shock itself would be exploited as comic relief, and its true relationship to the play be thereby obscured. Mr Eliot himself told me how fearsome was the effect produced by the Paris actors, for whom the clichés in the English text disappeared in translation and with them the comic element in the scene, and who played their apology with ferocious earnestness. Today, the devices of the 'thirties, such as the dinner-jackets under the heraldic cloaks employed in the production at Winchester College, are no longer necessary. We are accustomed nowadays to historical characters speaking in contemporary idiom, and the shock, like so many others which Mr Eliot has delivered, has helped to bring a dead patch in our imaginations to life again.

For the rest, this masterpiece is best served by a production which gives as simple a background as possible to the poet's words. This is one of the few dramas which have universal validity: it affects an audience in the same way whether in church or theatre, village schoolroom or air-raid shelter. Perhaps the limitations originally imposed by the Chapter House worked to this end upon the author's imagination. At any rate, experience shows that this play can always make its impact unless the producer gets in its way.

This is not so true of any of the remaining three plays, which represent Mr Eliot's attempt to make his own terms with the contemporary theatre. Here the producer has a more positive responsibility, for as Mr Eliot is using contemporary characters and scene with the object of bridging the gap between the modern audience and the people of his poetic drama, the producer must find ways of presenting the plays which seem as valid in visual terms as the dialogue aims to be in aural terms. This has for me involved a steady progression in style towards a patterned naturalism; a progression which I hope and believe may now have reached its end. For I believe that it is a dead end: though I am equally sure that that road, even if it is a cul-de-sac, was the necessary road for Mr Eliot to tread, and that his journey along it has been of a value to the theatre which only future generations will truly compute.

The Family Reunion stands now in a peculiar position in the canon of Mr Eliot's works. Many, perhaps most, of those who love his drama find this the most satisfying of his creations. Yet its author, acutely self-critical, is obsessed by its faults. In *Poetry and Drama* he points out, not for the first time, the faults of construction: the overlong exposition, and much more fundamental, 'a failure of adjustment between the Greek story and the modern situation'. But in his amusing criticism of 'those ill-fated figures, the Furies', he does not fully reveal the problem set to the producer. At the two climaxes of the play these figures have to be exposed to the leading character (who must be looking at them) and to the audience for a full minute (an eternity in the theatre), during which they neither speak nor move. This is the 'failure of adjustment' translated into theatrical terms: and will always prevent the climaxes of the play from attaining their object.

But for the rest, I believe that this play, which is indeed a half-way house for Mr Eliot between the ancient and the modern theatre, has more to give to a present-day audience than any he has written so far, and largely because it consists of an *effort* to adjust 'the Greek story' to 'the modern situation'. For the trouble with the purely modern poetic play is that its range of overtones is so limited. In producing *The Family Reunion* twice, I had a great advantage, for I learned a lot both from the first production and from life between 1939 and 1946.

In the first production I was concerned to establish a clear-cut style: to mark the transitions from the apparently naturalistic scenes to the Chorus of Uncles and Aunts (who a moment ago had been individual characters in those scenes) and back again; to give to the incantatory passages a ritual of their own; to ensure that the classic background should be affecting the audience during the whole of the play. Perhaps this severity, which was recently repeated in a West-End treatment, accounted for the fact that most of the play's audiences in 1939 felt separated from it, however much they admired it. One should add, however, that the public mood at the moment of the rape of Czechoslovakia was not congenial to such a play; whereas in 1946 it reflected much of our recent experience.

For in 1946 it seemed not at all difficult to pass from one convention in the play to another; and a production in which they melted into each other seemed to me much more satisfactory. There were cigarettes and sherry, chauffeur's and policeman's uniforms—and Harry's question whether the policeman was real seemed quite a natural one to those who had known the nightmares of the 1940's. Why not ask it naturally? And why then should not the elderly relations, when they had an overwhelming common concern for the family and for themselves, speak that concern in common? That the speech was labelled 'Chorus' in the text should make no difference. Why should not Agatha and Mary revolve in sad ritual round the memorial cake, praying rest for the dead whose birthday it had been, just as we file past the coffin of a great public figure? These things should not be separate from, but a full extension of, our modern life. The verse, flexibly modern in idiom yet as firm in rhythm as the Greek itself, set the style to the players, who found in their parts the full range of contemporary experience—which, after all, is a continuation of the heritage of the ages. The décor devised by Stella Mary Pearce for this production at the Mercury was based on the early eighteenth-century English country house, which gave a fully adequate suggestion of the classical. She unified the characters by dressing all the women in the same material, each keeping the same dress throughout the play with alterations of detail to effect the change from afternoon to evening.

The Cocktail Party followed two years after this second production and ten years after the completion of *The Family Reunion*. Even allowing for the gulf of the war, the nature of the impact which this play made is still surprising; for the first of its author's modern works had already made clear enough the direction in which he was heading. In the new play he moved a long way nearer to the style of the naturalistic stage. He carried the climactic experience of the hero of *The Family Reunion* onwards to show its results and its effects on those around his heroine in *The Cocktail Party*. In the process he discarded the Chorus, and almost surrendered his beloved 'runes'. Yet essentially the form is the same and the drama is as deeply poetic; the purport of the story is the same also, and as disturbing to all those who do not wish to go the author's way. The difference in effect is that, when that disturbance takes place, *The Cocktail Party* gives the audience no chance to insulate itself from the play's influence by saying to itself that it cannot recognize the characters or their situation as akin to its own.

In producing this play, and the one which followed it farther along the same road, my first duty to the author was, therefore, to make it as sure as I could that this recognition was made inevitable. Accordingly, in the setting for *The Cocktail Party*, Anthony Holland gave a good conventional Shaftesbury Avenue idea of a West-End flat and consulting-room—and nothing more. The actors were dressed by the same firms who would clothe any comedy shown on the London Theatre Guide; cigarettes were by Abdulla and stockings by Kayser Bondor. When the curtain rose on the chatter of the cocktail party no one who had not read the name of the author would suspect that anything out of the ordinary was going to happen on that stage.

The author was insistent that, at this particular moment in his career as a dramatist and in the development of poetic drama, this was the thing of first importance: and I have no doubt that he was right. For it must be remembered that neither of his two plays previously staged in London had reached the Shaftesbury Avenue public: *Murder in the Cathedral* had as the audience of its long success a public which seldom goes to the theatre at all, and *The Family Reunion* had been a failure in one off-West-End theatre and a success in another. *The Cocktail Party* did, in fact, draw the commercial theatre public both of New York and of London; the barrier was at last broken through.

Yet for the play this conventionally naturalistic treatment was inadequate. If I were doing it again today, I should want a setting which drew the imagination of the spectator beyond the external appearance, to look for 'the treasure' that Celia went into the forest to find, and to plumb the depths of the experience that only the play's poetry can convey. For Mr Eliot does himself an injustice when he says 'it is perhaps an open question whether there is any poetry in the play at all'. Its greatest virtue, to my mind, is that it integrates the poetic with the prosaic so firmly and convincingly.

To sustain this integration in performance was my principal aim. Rehearsals started accordingly with a period of reading through and through the play so that we should all have its rhythms embedded in our subconsciousness before we started to attempt the interpretation of its characters. I was immeasurably helped here by having Alec Guinness at the head of the original cast. His unfailingly accurate sensitiveness to the two levels of truth, poetic and natural, in the writing, and his genius in interpreting them (matched by that of Irene Worth as Celia and Cathleen Nesbitt as Julia), gave a lead which the rest of the cast followed successfully, so that the resultant performance had a style which unified the two levels of expression in the play. This production went from Edinburgh *via* Brighton to New York, where the acting certainly helped the play to become one of the landmarks in the post-war theatre. The London production was more often in danger of slipping towards the purely naturalistic: Rex Harrison's Reilly, a performance of brilliant polish, lacked that hieratic suggestion which Alec Guinness gave to the eccentricity of the modern Heracles, and Gladys Boot's Julia was a little too comfortable. But the play still emerged, on the whole, convincingly. The last act contains two passages which obstinately remain on one level only, the opening in which we find that the reconciliation of Edward and Lavinia has led to a complacently prosaic way of life, and the ending in which Reilly's expository speech sets off a train of pieties from the rest. But for these short lapses, *The Cocktail Party* seemed to me to remain poetic throughout, and thus to justify almost completely the author's determination to bring together his poetry and the current dramatic techniques.

In this and the following play the producer's most difficult problem was that of movement. Primacy must be given to the words: the audience's attention to them must not be disturbed by the physical action, which the poet has imagined less vividly than the dialogue. The action must be suitable; that is, it must be credible on the naturalistic level and yet must match the style of the words. This, in fact, means that it will be slower than in a naturalistic play, since much more is put into words by the poet than by the author who depends on the unspoken thought of real life. Today, the eye of an audience, trained by the movies, is much quicker than its ear, which has been made lazy by the facility of film dialogue and the ease with which its amplified words are heard. The eye, then, must be kept sufficiently satisfied for the relatively long time that the ear must take to hear fully what is being said. And the aim of this poet demands that the means adopted to satisfy the eye shall be consistent with the natural behaviour of the characters and not go beyond it.

It is interesting, and I think encouraging, to observe that criticism of these two successive attempts at poetic naturalism has tended to move towards rebellion against the restrictions of naturalistic behaviour. Since this criticism has come as much from the newspapers as from more academic sources, it seems to indicate that the theatre's public is ready for an advance into a wider territory: that, in fact, the poet's place in the theatre has been restored to him, to use as he, the poet, desires, and to justify in terms of a poetry which illuminates and universalizes the life of his characters. Most of those critics who hailed *The Confidential Clerk* as the best-constructed of Mr Eliot's modern plays (which it is) were also aware that just because he had mastered so many of the necessities of construction he had bound himself by them. This play conceals too effectively its deeper level, so that its audience tends to regard it as an enjoyably improbable fiction and never to become involved. Only in the scene between Colby and Lucasta at the beginning of Act II are the depths of loneliness suffered by the unwanted child opened to us, and the search for a 'garden' which is 'a part of one single world' is seen as the underlying motive of the play.

Could production do anything to bring this motive to light throughout the play, and to give the audience that unconscious awareness of the play's deeper level that alone fulfils the poet's aim? The two respects in which I aimed at doing this, and I hope to some extent fulfilled the aim, were in the décor and in the style of the acting. The settings to be shown were the Business Room in the private house of a financial magnate and Colby's flat in the mews. This time, it was not only admissible but desirable to add to the 'real' rooms with their necessary furnishings an extra dimension: Hutchinson Scott allowed us to look into the shadows behind the prosperous office and into the sky beyond the ceiling of the flat.

From establishing in our minds the verse-rhythms which pulsate beneath even the most prosaic of the utterances in *The Confidential Clerk*, we passed in rehearsal to the discovery of a style in which to play it. The plot, adapted from Euripides's *Ion*, produced a series of situations which seemed, on the naturalistic plane, increasingly improbable. They could in fact easily be paralleled in the real life of an age as sexually loose as our own; but on the stage they reminded one of Gilbert or—yes—of Oscar Wilde. Here was the right indication for the players: the verse which was for us by now the foundation of the play's being must be matched in its rhythm by a rhythm of performance akin to the high comedy of the writer to whom words are weapons, and manners the garment of feeling. Even though the feeling be far deeper, and the intention far greater, than those to be found in Wilde's plays, the style would be the right vehicle for them: and a unity of style was achieved by the London cast on this basis. That it counted for something in the effect which the play made upon audiences can be realized by comparing this with the result in New York. Here, a cast had been assembled which contained a number of strong personalities, each eminent in his or her own style of acting, and each differing widely from the other. Most of the resulting performances were good in themselves, but the play suffered from the lack of unity.

In *Poetry and Drama* Mr Eliot draws 'a triple distinction: between prose, and verse, and our ordinary speech which is mostly below the level of either verse or prose'. This distinction may serve to explain the difficulty which actors accustomed to naturalistic dialogue experience with a verse which includes naturalism in its scope without ceasing to be verse; and perhaps may provide a clue to its solution. One has to persuade most actors, however, to desire such a clue: for the actor, setting out to express himself through the impersonation of a character, seldom believes that the words given to him are the perfect, or even the primary, means to his end. He has to be convinced that the exact words chosen by the author, and in the case of a poet the exact rhythm in which the author heard those words, will do best what he as actor sets out to do. This conviction can be achieved with Mr Eliot's work, because he is precise in his use of words and because his taste and sensitivity are unfailing. To persuade actors of this, sometimes line by line, is the producer's most important task. Some will fight against it; others will at first be intimidated by the seeming restriction on their freedom of expression, and fear that they will never be able to bring a character to life. But any actor who has music in his soul will discover that in Mr Eliot's writing there is a measure of that perfection which he describes as the mirage before his eyes: 'a design of human action and of words, such as to present at once the two aspects of dramatic and of musical order'; and accordingly he will embrace his opportunity.

Only five works so far: and we all wait eagerly for the sixth. That has always been so: for Mr Eliot has always made us ask What Next? No writer is more securely grounded in tradition, nor is any more free from the restraints of convention. Since the war, he has voluntarily surrendered to certain stage conventions in order to achieve certain ends; that this surrender is not final is a postulate from the whole nature of his work. What Next, then?

I do not know: nor have I ever known. Throughout his period of work for the theatre I have enjoyed his friendship and been consulted during some part of the creative process that brought forth each play. Each new work has come as a fresh experience to me; each new impact has been unexpected. I have taken some time to appreciate its nature, and more time to understand how it should be presented on the stage. I conceive that the producer's task is that of interpreter: he should serve his author by finding the right terms in which to show his work on the stage, not by creating a work of his own. In that task, the producer needs to work at the author's own tempo; Mr Eliot's tempo is a slow one. And in the process of solving the detailed problems in the script, and of rehearsal, it is the quiet discussion, the thought spoken and left to germinate in the mind, that are of most use. With each play Mr Eliot has become more and more interested in the process of rehearsal and in the actor's approach to it; and his comments during that process have come to exercise a great influence on its development. A conscientious craftsman, he wrestles obstinately with the details of fitting his words to the actor's needs. Yet even when in the theatre he is not of it; and one is conscious that the influence which he has exercised through this tiny corpus of playwriting is of a wider nature: he restores to the drama a dimension which it has lost in a theatre become ingrown, the dimension of that life which through the drama we should have more abundantly.

Interpreting Becket and Other Parts

ROBERT SPEAIGHT

IT WAS a sunny morning early in May 1935 when I received a letter from my friend, Martin Browne, inviting me to play the part of Becket in *Murder in the Cathedral.* The invitation was a tempting one. I was a recent convert to Eliot's poetry and I knew him personally. We used to meet at Lady Ottoline Morrell's, and he had been a faithful member of the Old Vic audience when I was acting there in the season of 1931–32. I had seen *The Rock* performed at Sadler's Wells in a production by Martin Browne, and I had seen *Sweeney Agonistes* brilliantly interpreted by Rupert Doone at the Westminster. The choruses from *The Rock* and the whole of *Sweeney* were as satisfying as anything one had listened to on the modern stage. A new play about the murder of Becket acted in the Chapter House of Canterbury Cathedral only a few yards from the site of his martyrdom was a chance that no young actor would want to miss, and since the play was written by the most discussed poet of the day there could be no doubt of my answer. I telegraphed my acceptance even before I had read the text.

It so happened that I was due to leave that same afternoon for Rome, where I was attending, in the temporary capacity of newspaper correspondent, the ceremonies of canonization for John Fisher and Thomas More. I carried in my pocket the version of *Murder in the Cathedral* which Eliot had specially prepared for the Canterbury performance. Since these performances were not supposed to last for more than an hour and forty minutes, certain cuts had been made, and the antiphonal opening to the second part, which suited the semi-liturgical setting of the Chapter House, was printed here instead of the Chorus which afterwards replaced it. By the time I was comfortably ensconced in the Rome Express and the train was racing through Picardy, I was ready to concentrate on the part which had just been offered to me.

My initial feeling was one of vague disappointment. There could be no doubt of the play's originality, nor of the beauty of the choral writing. But where was Becket? He appeared to me a very passive protagonist. Assailed by the tempters, importuned by the Chorus, harassed by the Priests and murdered by the Knights, he had little to do—or so it seemed—but go forward to a predetermined fate. The best poetry of the play had not been put into his mouth, and the long sermon in which he explained his slightly equivocal victory over spiritual pride was written in so colloquial a prose that its dramatic significance escaped me. This Becket, I thought, was more of a figure than a part; and if the figure was what counted, then I had no need of a mirror to tell me that I lacked much of the five foot six inches of the man whom it took four assassins to kill. This want of stature always bothered me, but I think Ivor Brown was the only critic to point it out.

I am a bad reader of plays, and it was only in rehearsal that the full dimensions of the part began to reveal themselves. It was true that the Becket of *Murder in the Cathedral* was a man more acted upon than acting, but there was a tremendous force in his passivity. His submitted will had the strength and resilience of steel. It was true that the play was more—or less—than the story of Becket; it was a play about the making of a saint, with a rich contemporary relevance, and this had its own fascination. It was true that Becket was an idea rather than a character, but there was a strong challenge in clothing the idea with flesh and blood. It was true that, as Granville Barker afterwards said in his Romanes Lecture, *Murder in the Cathedral* came very close to liturgical drama; but even liturgy must have some relation to life and it was up to me to establish it. Here the dramatic force of the sermon struck me as soon as I had started to memorize it. The hieratic figure of the first act, with its rather laboured retrospections and its calm looking forward to martyrdom, imprisoned by the stiff rhythms of the verse—a part, it seemed, of some Byzantine pattern which no touch of naturalism must be allowed to break—now became human and approachable. In stepping up to the pulpit

Becket stepped down from the pedestal, and the actor was given a single opportunity for pathos.

I always had a strong instinct that Becket should show signs of emotion when he told his people—here it was the Chorus and the audience and Dr Cosmo Gordon Lang in the front row—that he would probably never preach to them again. That is the kind of instinct that actors tend to have, but when I came later to write my biography of Becket, I found that, as a matter of historical record, Becket's control had entirely broken down at this point. Some people always held that the Becket of *Murder in the Cathedral* would never have faltered; others, among whom was Harold Hobson writing in the *Sunday Times*, regarded this as the best thing in my performance. Generally speaking, the more an actor is moved himself, the less he will move his audience; but there are exceptions to this, and perhaps I was right. However, when I saw Alec Guinness play the part of the Cardinal in *The Prisoner*, I wondered if I had been wrong.

The circumstances of our first performance of *Murder in the Cathedral* were picturesque, but they were not easy. It was impressive to hear the Knights thundering on the oaken doors of the Chapter House and to watch them stamping down the aisle between the spectators, seated on their uncomfortable wooden chairs. It was impressive to be carried out into the Great Cloister preceded by the Chorus, with their lighted candles, chanting the Litany of the Saints. It was provocative to find oneself in an Elizabethan proximity to one's audience, with no curtain and next to no lighting to cut one off. But the acoustics of the Chapter House are not good; the voices get lost in the vaulting and one always has to speak with the brake on. The building has a certain Gothic bleakness, which was suitable enough to the play but which somehow forbade enjoyment. And all plays, even religious plays, are meant to be enjoyed. *Murder in the Cathedral* proved its power on many stages; in the little Mercury Theatre at Notting Hill Gate, where Ashley Dukes gave it its first London showing; at the Duchess and at the Old Vic; in many provincial theatres and in front of the West Front at Tewkesbury. But nowhere, I think, was it so effective as at the Mercury. Here there was an excellent 'apron' which allowed the Chorus to deploy; and the theatre, though it was inconveniently small, somehow left room for big acting. It had, in fact, only one serious fault: there was no seat big enough to accommodate G. K. Chesterton when he wanted to see the play.

I have acted Becket more than a thousand times in Great Britain, Ireland, Canada and the United States, and I suppose I am expected to say that I never got tired of it. But this would be quite untrue. I doubt if it is good for any actor to go on playing a part for as long as this, even though his performances are not consecutive. He gets fixed in a certain style, and the public imagines that he can play no other kind of part. Ivor Brown once referred to me as 'immured in the crypt of St Eliot's', and the words contained a dreadful truth. For many years I was destined to a line of parts—a long procession of ecclesiastics—and the shadow of Becket overhung them all. The truth is that while I am interested in religion, I have no particular preference for religious drama. I would far rather play Falstaff or Sir Toby Belch. Nor am I one of those actors who can devote all their energies to the repetition of the same performance; I am interested in too many other things. This may very well be a weakness, but I know that I often turned on my performance of Becket like a gramophone record, and sometimes the needle got stuck. I needed the stimulus of a special occasion or a new stage or a fresh cast if I were to recover my initial enthusiasm. It was easy to lie back, so to speak, on the strong rhythms of the verse instead of getting on top of them; easy to let one's mind drift away completely from what one's voice was saying. And when this happened the record had a fatal tendency to slow down. The fault, I am well aware, was my own; but if the rhythm of the part had not been so stiff and, on occasion, so incantatory, I think that I should have been able to keep myself more flexible.

The difficulty of acting in *Murder in the Cathedral* was similar to the difficulty of acting in Shakespeare, but it was not the same. In each case the actor must create the illusion of life within a poetic convention. He must animate, but he must not transgress, the rhythms of the verse which the author has put into his mouth. Whereas, however, the characters in Shakespeare are manifestly flesh and blood, in Becket the flesh and blood had to be recovered and assumed. Becket, from his first entrance, stands on the threshold of his doom, and only now and then does he look back, with a twinge of nostalgia, to the days of his temporal glory; his supremacy as Chancellor, his efficient administration and his challenge to the feudal powers. These moments had to be caught and emphasized. Another Becket had to be recalled from an abdicated past; the audience had to feel the strength and vividness of a fleeting retrospect. And unless one was on the top of one's toes, the opportunity was missed. If the Becket of *Murder in the Cathedral* were to remain human and comprehensible, one had to withstand—without hostility—certain tendencies of the play. It was easy to become automatic; and there is no place for automation on the stage.

My interest in the part, and in the play, was given a new lease of life when I was invited to act it in French. This invitation came to me from the Théâtre des Compagnons in Montreal, and I was invited to direct the play as well as act in it. My production did not differ, essentially, from Martin Browne's, which I had greatly admired and to which I owed so much; but there were a few innovations. I preached the sermon without a pulpit and in the full pontifical vestments which Becket would have worn at the Midnight Mass. This was one of those occasions when theatrical truth and liturgical accuracy had seemed to be in conflict. But when the liturgists told me that in the twelfth century Archbishops wore vestments of whatever colour they fancied, it occurred to me that Becket might well have chosen the red of martyrdom—even on Christmas Eve. I had feared lest the simplicity of the sermon might be spoiled if Becket were too splendidly attired. But I am sure that the red chasuble had a dramatic effect, and that the absence of a pulpit counteracted its formality.

The French-Canadian actors with whom I worked were new to Eliot, but they gave an excellent account of themselves and the play was especially successful in Quebec. The taste of Montreal was too trivial for such austere fare. I had never acted in French before, but I found no difficulty in learning my part afresh in Henri Fluchère's excellent translation, and I quickly felt as if this was how I had always played it. When one is attacking a part for the first time, I think it is nearly always a mistake to direct the play oneself; and when one has worked out an interpretation with a director in whom one has confidence, it is extremely difficult to give one's confidence to someone else. That is one reason why it was probably a good thing for me not to have played Becket on the screen. But when one knows a play and a part as well as I had come to know *Murder in the Cathedral*, I think it is both salutary and stimulating to be given complete authority. I have not played Becket since I played him in French, and I have never enjoyed playing him more. I have also acted the part several times on radio and television, and here I relished the opportunities, without being irked by the limitations, of a new medium. In the sermon I was preaching to a much larger audience than I had ever addressed in the theatre; yet I was able to speak to them in a voice lowered almost to a whisper, and I found that the text lent itself perfectly to this confidential treatment.

Eliot's second play, *The Family Reunion*, is, in my opinion, his best; but I have never been closely associated with it. I was in New York when it came out and I remember a Sunday-afternoon reading by a number of actors, none of whom—myself included—had the faintest notion what it was about. Well, we have all grown up to *The Family Reunion* since then, although, as far as I know, the play has never been given in New York. On one occasion I was invited by Radio Eireann to play Harry Monchensey, and there I enjoyed speaking over the air a part that I could never have acted on the stage. Certain scenes I also acted in French over the radio in Paris. These formed part of a programme in honour of T. S. Eliot, who had just been awarded the Nobel Prize for Literature. This very limited experience in the part of Harry Monchensey taught me that when a man talks so incessantly about himself the only way to save him from appearing a tiresome prig is to make him a good deal more theatrical than he seems to be on paper. We do not get tired of Hamlet, because Hamlet is always behaving in an exciting way, and there is little risk of one's underplaying him. But the mood of *The Family Reunion*, like the mood of *Murder in the Cathedral*, is so retrospective that immediacy is easily lost, and I felt it to be essential that the two scenes of Harry's encounter with the Eumenides should be whipped up to a high pitch of theatrical excitement. The second of these encounters follows his conversion, a conversion which is the climax of the play. But the climax is only made theatrically audible, so to speak, when Harry shows that, at last, he can face his pursuers without fear. Both in the English and the French versions I tried to play these scenes for perhaps a shade more than they were worth.

The great conquest of *The Family Reunion* was a style of verse which achieved colloquial ease and also, when required, a high poetic incandescence. If I am lecturing on the modern poetic drama, I always quote the scene between Charles and Downing as a perfect example of the former. If this is read or acted as it should be, the audience will hardly be aware that they are listening to verse, and yet, as the scene progresses, will feel that they are not listening to prose. How superbly the more poetic passages are fitted to stage delivery was shown by Henrietta Watson's extraordinary performance as Lady Monchensey. Nothing finer in tragic acting has been seen on the London stage in my recollection. The echoes of her last scene linger like the poet's own farewell to the grand manner, for in his next play Eliot was working to a comic, not to a tragic, pattern. There is tragedy as well as comedy in *The Cocktail Party*; but if it is straining language to describe this play as a comedy, there is hardly any strain in describing its successor as farce. I have never acted in *The Cocktail Party*, although the part of Harcourt-Reilly strongly tempts me, but I did play in *The Confidential Clerk*. No sooner had I started to master the dry, staccato rhythms of Sir Claude Mulhammer than I realized the distance that Eliot had travelled since *Murder in the Cathedral*. Was it a step forward or a step back? It was, in any case, a step aside.

I did not greatly enjoy acting in *The Confidential Clerk*. I had read it in manuscript and seen it on the stage, but even there, in spite of a brilliant cast, it had seemed to me no more than a dramatic exercise on five fingers. Distinguished but dry, it hovered uneasily between prophecy and farce. I was less disturbed by the disappearance of the poetry than I was disappointed by the stiffness of the prose. Except for a single scene with the young man he believes to be his son, Sir Claude Mulhammer is not a particularly good part. But the key of comedy in which it must be played imposes on this scene a speed which I could not help feeling diminished its effect. If so tight a tycoon as Sir Claude were so far to unbutton himself as to confess to a frustrated vocation for ceramics, he would surely have done so to a slower, more broken rhythm. As it was, one felt the spurs in one's flank, goading one on to the last two acts where one had little to do except to be an efficient cog in a machine which seemed much too mechanical.

I cannot pretend to admire the plays of Eliot as much as I admire his poetry, and the interpretation of his poetry has given me more pleasure than the interpretation of any of his parts—Becket himself not excepted. I had the privilege of reading the last three Quartets over the radio as they came out, and I have twice recorded them for long-playing on the gramophone. The first recording left me dissatisfied; as I heard it played back I felt that my reading was much too slow. Here was the old temptation of a contemplative text which had sometimes caught me out in the sermon from *Murder in the Cathedral.* I was very grateful, therefore, when the Argo Record Company invited me to make a second recording, and I was astonished at how much time I was able to save in a reading which, even then, seemed quite unhurried. It was otherwise with *The Waste Land.* This I still regard as the summit of Eliot's poetry, and far more dramatic—I am almost tempted to say far more theatrical—than anything that he has written for the stage. Here there was an opportunity for impersonation—Madame Sosostris, the voices in the pub, the bank clerk, the couple in the canoe—richer than anything in the plays. The rhythms of the poem had a variety which I have discovered nowhere else except in Shakespeare. It was a fascinating challenge to interpret this variety without losing hold of the poet's integrating vision, and without dissipating the concentration which had made so marvellous a melody out of so much deliberate dissonance, so intricately organized a poem out of so many fragments.

If Eliot's drama had developed on the lines of *The Waste Land*—the speculation is vain but, for me, continuously haunting. In *Sweeney Agonistes* there were signs that it might have done so. On one or two occasions I have read the whole of this poem aloud, although—in contrast, I think, to *The Waste Land*—it needs the percussion of several voices. (One of these occasions was in Colombo, where practically everyone is called Pereira, and where the banyan trees composed an embarrassing background.) The syncopated rhythms of *Sweeney*, like the sophisticated dialogue of *The Waste Land*, announced the possibility of a new poetic drama which should be at once timeless and contemporary. So indeed it has turned out, but meanwhile the Liturgy and the Greeks and the well-made play have interposed their several conventions. T. S. Eliot has arrived in Shaftesbury Avenue and the English actor owes him much. But if he had chosen to go elsewhere, I think that gratitude might have been even greater.

A Postscript from Mrs Chamberlayne and Mrs Guzzard

ALISON LEGGATT

I ARRIVED at the first rehearsal of the London production of *The Cocktail Party* with a feeling of apprehension—'my damp soul sprouting despondently'—and I was quite frankly relieved when I discovered that Mr Eliot was not going to be present! Other than Shakespeare, I had never acted in a play in verse, and I doubted my capabilities. This tension, however, was relaxed by the genial arrival of Mr Henry Sherek, our manager, with his gifts of flower-sprays for the women of the cast.

As rehearsals progressed my fears left me, for the verse, far from inhibiting, carried one along with its wonderful flow and rhythm, and I found the learning of words easier than in ordinary plays.

One day we heard that Mr Eliot was to be in front during rehearsal and there was naturally a feeling of nervousness among the cast. But our worries were soon set at ease, and a gentler, kinder and more considerate author could not be imagined.

Our producer had advised us not to ask our dramatist to explain any lines that we might find obscure. However, one member of the cast, splendidly daring, disregarded this advice and asked: 'Please, what does this mean?'—to receive the reply: 'My dear child, don't ask me, I don't know!'

When I was rehearsing for *The Confidential Clerk* I ventured to seek a little guidance over the part of Mrs Guzzard, which I was playing. 'She is a mixture of Pallas Athene and a suburban housewife,' Mr Eliot told me!

I found great help from our producer, Mr Martin Browne, who

had a flair for explaining to us which word, or phrase, in any speech called for focus or high-lighting.

And then we arrived at the first night—chic, intelligent, alarming and exciting—to be encouraged with the most delightful messages on the bouquets from the author: mine read, 'The Perfection of Guzzards', a beautifully human touch that took away all my nervousness and made me laugh! Afterwards we all felt very relaxed at the gay party which he gave us.

It was later, during those two successful West-End runs, that the real delight of being in an Eliot play became so apparent. The stimulation stayed with us all the time—every evening and every matinée.

We were continually caught up in discussion with friends from the audience—those that 'raved', and those that didn't understand; those that liked *The Cocktail Party* more than *The Confidential Clerk*, and vice versa. I remember one eminent clergyman telling me that the second act of *The Cocktail Party* was the finest sermon on Repentance that he had ever encountered.

And we, saying those lines daily, were kept on the alert all the while. The spirit of the plays allowed for no relaxation or slackness, and I can honestly say that acting in them one learnt undiscovered truths in one's parts all the time.

Then, towards the end of each run, we all received from our author copies of each play charmingly inscribed.

For the suburban Pallas Athene
Alison Leggatt—in gratitude.

T. S. ELIOT

read my treasured copy of *The Confidential Clerk*. And these books remain as lovely souvenirs of two of the high-lights of my theatrical career.

Filming *Murder in the Cathedral*

GEORGE HOELLERING

FOR many years after I had produced my Hungarian film, *Hortobagy*, I was looking for a suitable work by a modern poet. What I wanted to do was to combine verse and image in a similar way in which I had combined music and image in *Hortobagy*—a film where attention would be focused on the verse and the audience would have to listen as well as to look.

After a long search, I found my subject in Mr Eliot's *Murder in the Cathedral.* I approached him about the film rights and explained to him the kind of film I had in mind. Though he had no great respect for films in general, Mr Eliot was interested in my idea. I had the impression that he saw here a possibility of experimenting with verse in a new medium. It is this constant readiness to experiment with language and dramatic forms that has kept Mr Eliot so fresh and youthful as a writer. He was quite unconcerned about the financial aspects; what mattered to him were the artistic standards. I therefore showed him some examples of my previous work, and also offered to prepare a complete film adaptation of the play before asking him to come to a decision.

After a few months I sent Mr Eliot the completed adaptation. He was very pleased with it and agreed to give me the film rights, subject to contract. In the contract he was given the right to approve the cast, the music, the costumes and sets, as well as each day's 'rushes' and the final version of the film. To grant an author such far-reaching rights is a risky business for a producer; Mr Eliot might have objected to many things, not only in the course of the production but also when the film had been completed, which would have endangered all the capital invested in the film.

I managed, however, to convince my financial backers that this was an advantage rather than a risk, since it would help to ensure that the film would authentically represent Mr Eliot's work on the screen. I had gained this conviction in many talks about the production with Mr Eliot, and, more particularly, through listening to him reading his own verse.

A further advantage of my granting Mr Eliot these rights was that it associated him more closely with the production. He took a great personal interest in everything that was going on, and I could always judge from his reactions whether or not I was proceeding along the right lines. I almost blush to think how much of Mr Eliot's time I took up during that period with my queries and discussions—time that was always given freely and willingly.

During the work on the script, and after listening to some of Mr Eliot's poetry recordings, I began to feel that it would be ideal if Mr Eliot could record the whole play in his own voice—a recording that would be authoritative as regards rhythm, stress and variations of tone. I explained to him that such a recording would be of great value to me: (*a*) as a kind of 'piano score' of the whole, complex interplay of voices, for my own use; (*b*) as a guide for the actors; and (*c*) as a guide for the composer of the music, which was to be minutely geared to the rhythm and tone of the verse.

Mr Eliot was pleased with this idea. He had experienced difficulties with actors and producers before, over the proper delivery of his verse, and was glad to see that I attached such paramount importance to this point. He agreed, and for several months came regularly once a week to a little recording studio in St John's Wood (this was still during the Flying Bomb period), where he read through the entire play in his careful and precise voice. The recording sessions finally produced 16,000 feet of film, and with one exception no re-recordings were necessary, as Mr Eliot prepared himself for each session with meticulous care, even learning large stretches of the play by heart. The one repetition that did become necessary was not his fault, or rather, it was his writing and not his speaking that was responsible for it. When, towards the end of the play, we came to the speeches in which the three Knights justify themselves before the crowd, the sound recordist suddenly turned round to Mr Eliot and, completely forgetting his control switches, said excitedly, 'Aren't they right, sir? What do you think?' Mr Eliot, needless to say, was highly amused.

I found, during these recording sessions, that Mr Eliot was not only the best interpreter of his own verse—which is not always the case with poets—but also had the makings of a very able actor. It was fascinating to listen to him recording the murder of the Archbishop—to the masterly way in which he contrasted the brutal, drunken voices of the Knights with the calm, humble voice of Becket. I was so enthusiastic over these recordings that I went a little too far in my demands on Mr Eliot and asked him to play the part of Becket himself. He was not at all annoyed by the suggestion, in fact I think he was even a little tempted, but he finally turned down the suggestion. During our discussions on this point, I was, however, able to explain to him that I felt the Fourth Tempter should not be treated as a visual figure, but as a disembodied voice, and to ask him to speak the part in the film. In spite of all his other work at the time, he had by then become so involved in the making of the film that, to my great joy, he finally agreed. The result fully came up to my expectations. His delivery of this part has an inner quality that will outlive any style of acting.

During the shooting Mr Eliot frequently came to the studio, and any small alterations could be settled there and then. He always showed unfailing patience and helpfulness. Only over one point were there any difficulties, and for these I must take the responsibility. I found it difficult to express in filmic terms the speeches of the Knights after the murder, and explained to Mr Eliot that, in my opinion, the whole atmosphere of this part of the film would suffer if the Knights suddenly started to address the audience at length at this point. The effect would not be the same as on the stage, and I would prefer to make the point of these speeches in a more indirect way. 'You mean', said Mr Eliot, 'that it would be a *Stilbruch*' (an untranslatable German word, meaning a sudden, inartistic change of style). When I replied 'Yes', he said that this scene was his main reason for writing the play, and that the only way he could see to get his point across was for the Knights to address the audience directly. I madc several alternative suggestions, and Mr Eliot finally accepted one of them. The point here was that, following the murder of Becket, the people of Canterbury had been shown realistically and in action, preparing to storm the Cathedral. The Knights were therefore placed in a position where they had to act quickly and decisively; it would have completely interrupted the continuity of the film to let them deliver at this point the long, ironic speeches of the play, which are really addressed to the audience and not to the people of Canterbury. *Afterwards* it was possible for a brief moment 'out of time' to turn round and explicitly confront the cinema audience with a short speech, and this Mr Eliot wrote specially for the film. I still feel, however, that this was the weakest part of the film, and that here I failed Mr Eliot. I lost some of the typical clownery and ironical humour of these speeches, and so the scene, as it stands, has too political a flavour. If I could re-make the film, I think that I would now be able to solve this problem more satisfactorily.

Mr Eliot's work on the film did not even stop with the world première at Venice (where it received the prizes for the Best Film in Costume and the Best Art Direction) and the London première. Watching the film in cinemas with big popular audiences, I realized that some of the choruses would come across better if they were differently illustrated, and also that the film needed to be somewhat shortened, since even intelligent audiences found it difficult to swallow complex poetry in such concentrated doses. In the theatre there are always the intervals. So I provided some new illustrations and re-edited a number of scenes, which Mr Eliot again checked in detail and with great care. I may add that all this sacrifice of time and effort was entirely voluntary on Mr Eliot's part.

As the reader may have gathered by now, the making of *Murder in the Cathedral* was not an easy task. I should like to end by expressing my gratitude to Mr Eliot for making the time I spent on the film the happiest and most stimulating of my career.

Televising *The Cocktail Party*

MICHAEL BARRY

FOUR of Mr T. S. Eliot's plays have been seen on B.B.C. television: *Murder in the Cathedral*, *The Family Reunion*, *The Cocktail Party* and *The Confidential Clerk*. One of these, *The Cocktail Party*, will be discussed here. It must be remembered that the plays were written for production in the theatre or, in the case of *Murder in the Cathedral*, for the Chapter House at Canterbury, and that they were striving after a new form and pattern of expression. Because of this, the preparation of *The Cocktail Party* for the television screen presented particular problems. I will try and outline the way in which we sought to overcome these.

The playwright in the theatre creates with great care a complex pattern of thoughts, words and movements to be seen and heard on a three-dimensional stage by the human eye and ear. The television screen presents a series of two-dimensional pictures seen by optical lenses which possess characteristics quite different from the eye. They alter the physical aspects of dimension, so that not only is the illusion of distance between the audience and the players different, but the ratio of prominence between the players themselves and the players and their surroundings assume an altered significance. The same applies to the reproduction of sound, although this is at first less apparent. The scientist interprets these factors as a mathematical problem. The producer finds them a handicap only in so far as they are misunderstood and misused, for there are ways in which they may be used to penetrate and illuminate. Perhaps the result that must chiefly be kept in mind is that the pictures themselves, by their juxtaposition and sequence, impose a visual pattern or rhythm. A poet like Mr Eliot is already using not one, but two rhythms in performance—the aural rhythm of his words and the rhythm or pattern of the thoughts beneath the words. The imposition, therefore, of a third pattern, strongly dominant and in effect more positive than, for instance, the movements the theatre producer gives to his actors, must be made with a complete understanding of the need to integrate, it might also be said to orchestrate, the whole.

I remember the sense of excitement after first seeing *The Cocktail Party* in the theatre. A sense of having watched a masterly diagnosis in which the poet, freed from the trammels of ordinary dialogue, had stripped the layers of sensibility that prohibit complete communication. I will not, however, pretend that this feeling persisted throughout the evening. A point was reached when what I called at the time mental indigestion set in, and this in turn sent one to the theatre again and to the text of the play for a fuller understanding.

Some time later, the play was cast for television, and owing to the sudden illness of the producer I had to join the script and company on the first day of rehearsal. This was in January 1952, when we were still transmitting with the limited resources of the old Alexandria Palace studios, and our efforts were perhaps no more than a sketch, a preparation for another production. The number of viewers was about 3,500,000, and I resolved at that time when circumstances improved we should ask Mr Eliot to allow us to present his play again.

This opportunity occurred in April 1957, and this time we reached eight million viewers—about twenty-one per cent of the adult population. We had the advantage of Mr Henry Sherek's theatre knowledge, and he had prepared a version to run for ninety minutes that was approved by the author. Why was the text shortened? My intention was to bring the spectator closely into the play. He would be present in the same room, sitting at the same desk as the players. He would look across a shoulder and perceive immediately the tremor of an eyelid on occasions when a speech might be required to carry the same meaning to the back of a theatre dress-circle. The sum of many such speeches could vitiate the heightened concentration that was going to be television's unique contribution.

Before any movement was plotted in *The Cocktail Party*, we sat and read the play until the company were accustomed to each other's voices and to the rhythms of the text. I did not pre-plan, as is usual, the movement of cameras and actors in detail beforehand. On this occasion it seemed most important to ensure that these movements should emphasize and accent the patterns already established by the author and not interrupt them. The ground-plan allowed considerable flexibility for deploying equipment, and this provided freedom to develop, as rehearsals progressed, the kind of camera-work I believed right for this production.

The cocktail party itself I saw as a close-knit pattern of movement in the middle of which would be the spectator, looking first this way and then that, seeking, like the other guests in the opening scene, an explanation for the presence of the Unknown Guest, whose figure, strongly blocked in the foreground, would dominate the opening sequence. Thereafter the spectator would be present in the room, which, by the nature of the camera-shots used, would seem to enclose him with the players. They, because of this nearness, need employ no theatrical emphasis to communicate across a distance with their audience. The opportunity that television offers to read the eyes and watch the mind anticipate words seemed valuable to our purpose. More immediate understanding is possible when this is properly used. Celia's search to understand Edward's thought in the second scene, the groping *rencontre* of the Chamberlaynes after their consultation with Harcourt-Reilly and the whole of his long discourse with Celia become intimacies quietly observed.

In order to obtain the necessary access into the larger of the two sets, the Chamberlaynes' flat, this was planned to be open on two sides, an L-shaped room. Furthermore, I wished the playing area to be away from the walls, which have a habit of crowding in on television actors, without at the same time designing a set that would appear vast when looked at by the wider lenses. Mr Stephen Taylor obtained this by putting on one side a deep recess, low-ceilinged and backed by wide windows, and on the other a barred partition through which one looked at the door beyond. The set had an open, contemporary air, but at the same time created a feeling of confinement about the Chamberlaynes' life. Let it not be thought that any profound symbolism was intended by the décor, which was first and always a background for the characters of the play, but, as I said earlier, the composition of each picture compels a significance that must be planned and used, or rejected, as part of the overall pattern.

The same importance attaches to the visual manipulation of the players within the frame, but success in this, the technical side of production, is measured by its apparent absence. The spectator should be oblivious of any intervention between himself and what is taking place on the screen. He should be conscious only that his attention is held, his eye satisfied and his senses stirred, but in order to bring this about a lot of careful work must take place. A use of composition and movement within the frame to allow the play-wright's emphases to be restated in terms of the screen, a pattern and punctuation in the picture sequence that flows with the content of the play. There exists a grammar in this matter, subject, as in writing, to a variety of styles. The style may be considered all important. The work of an author of the quality of T. S. Eliot offers a challenge, but one that possesses a distinction infinitely rewarding to accept.

Setting *The Hollow Men* to Music

DENIS ApIVOR

I HAVE been asked to write something about the problems of setting T. S. Eliot's poetry to music, with special reference to *The Hollow Men*. Yet, curiously enough, I have few memories of the actual creation of this work, which seems at a distance of nearly twenty years to have been almost automatic.

A remarkable feature, which must immediately strike a musician, is the music-like mode of construction employed by the poet in *The Hollow Men*. The effect is not impressionistic, as, for instance, are certain parts of Joyce's *Finnegans Wake*, but the poem employs, deliberately or unconsciously, musical devices—in reality, variations on thematic fragments—which form the basis of the art of composition. What a composer does in the way of subtle variation—augmentation, diminution, inversion, echoes, mirror-images and reappearances for dramatic effect—is the method used by Mr Eliot in his theme of 'death's kingdom'; 'lost kingdoms'; 'death's other kingdom'; 'death's twilight kingdom'; 'death's dream kingdom'; and '*For Thine is the Kingdom*'.

Woven into his word-music, too, are the themes of the eyes that are direct; that he 'dare not meet in dreams'; that reappear and are absent. Then again there are the broken columns, stone images and broken stones; the fading and dying stars; the sound of the wind and dried voices; the rat's feet over broken glass and the rat's coat blowing about the crossed staves of the scarecrow—these all become part of the litany of frustration, whose response is repeated three times:

Falls the Shadow.

It becomes clear very quickly, therefore, that this kind of verse imposes its own musical form very precisely. Moreover, Mr Eliot introduces a dominating dramatic device in the distorted version of 'Here we go round the mulberry bush', whose effect is heightened by music so that it seems as if the whole poem and its setting both derive from it and lead up to it. In fact, a key to the musical setting of the poem could be found in the combination of vulgar secular (jazz) rhythms with the solemnity of liturgical chant, and this is the way which I approached the problem of setting such verse which is already *half-way to music*.

An accurate description of the music itself without music-type can hardly be attempted here, but certain points may be worth noting.[1] The poet's personal and impersonal voices are retained by using a baritone solo and male-voice chorus respectively. It is the orchestra—specially chosen for certain timbres, and consisting of five wood-wind, two saxophones, six brasses, percussion, piano and strings—which opens the work, with a twisted (chromatic) version of the 'Mulberry Bush' tune: five notes, of which the last three, descending, accompany throughout the idea of the 'falling shadow' and the 'fading star'. In inversion this fragment suggests the squeaking of rats, and in augmentation the idea of stone images, the supplicating hand. What I have referred to as the litany of frustration is first heard in monotone at the words:

Shape without form

and its accompaniment of descending chords is maintained at its reappearance in the final section:

Between the idea
And the reality.

The second section beginning:

Eyes I dare not meet in dreams

starts both slowly and sadly with sliding chromaticisms reminiscent of 'blues harmony', and reaches a climax on rhythms derived from jazz suggesting momentarily the aimlessness of the wind. There follows the third section of the work, which is musically a palindrome accompanied by strings. The imagery of the desert, the stone images

[1] The score is published by the Oxford University Press, 1951.

and the supplicating hand coincides momentarily with an image from the fifth part of *The Waste Land*—'Then spoke the thunder'. In the fourth section the solemn chorus which begins:

The eyes are not here

is accompanied by striding *pizzicati* basses and clicking castanets and xylophones. This section terminates with a spoken stanza against a percussion accompaniment suggestive of waves breaking on a distant shore. The fifth and last section has an instrumental introduction in jazz rhythm, and the last trombones simultaneously declaim the solemn chorale, *Eine Feste Burg*. The climax of the music is the 'Mulberry Bush' tune in various guises, to which Mr Eliot's words are declaimed by the chorus. One of these variants is a cynical harmonization by Peter Warlock. The dance disappears in reiterated *sforzandi* and the litany begins, the musical elements of which I have touched on already. In the last ten bars the rhythmic motto appears momentarily in the bass strings, like a feebly beating heart, and the soloist speaks the last stanza against a sad whisp of melody on a single flute.

Eleven years after the completion of this work, I returned to the musical inspiration of Mr Eliot's verse in *Landscapes*—set this time for one singer, and a small group of instruments—and have on one occasion been seduced by his humorous cat-poems, which have been set more extensively by other composers recently. I believe that as a composer, as apart from a reader of verse, I shall return again and again to scan his work; for to me no poet writing in English this century can offer the equal of his musicality, his sonorous lyricism and his dramatic impact. But as I grow older my inhibitions against setting verse of this calibre multiply. Indeed, the attitude of any musician tempted to set Mr Eliot's verse should perhaps be expressed best in the words of Mr Prufrock:

'Do I dare?' and, 'Do I dare?'

Reading T. S. Eliot with Schoolboys

HUGH DINWIDDY

THE simplicity of poetry brings pain and joy, and a deepening knowledge of reality to the listener. When the listener is a boy at school whose education is for ever urging him towards a state of being grown-up, there is a particular kind of protecting unreality to dissolve before poetry can have meaning for him. On the one hand he is being trained to be strong, independent, resourceful and practical, and on the other to be attentive to the profound realities of poetry, which ask for a state of silence, of stillness within the listener.

No one can read T. S. Eliot's poetry with understanding unless he is aware that he is listening to a voice, like music, speaking out of silence. The act of faith, then, which one makes before reading him to the young, is that everyone has been born with the gift of silence, and that, however obscured it may be by daily and habitual activism, it can be touched into receptivity by the grace of words. Now that everyone is being educated up to the hilt, resistance against the schoolmaster's voice is strong, and I have been pleased on many occasions with the response of boys who have enjoyed readings of Eliot when they have remarked that 'it didn't seem like a class'. Indeed, poetry is to be shared with friends, and only thus can it become part of one's growing-up, and not, in modern terms, just another class.

We have now a generation of schoolboys who have, in fact, grown up with Eliot's poetry, who have had him in their desks, have been led by ardent schoolmasters to performances of his plays and who may be said to be able to recognize Mrs Equitone when they see her. In so far as his work is contemporary and analytical of society, it is now easy to share in a wide circle of friends. It invites comment, and it enlarges the circle with popular figures of satire. Its simplicity and unobtrusive skill have, of course, drawn from boy listeners varying kinds of praise, many distinctly back-handed, such as the over-frequent 'it doesn't seem like poetry', which is followed by the inevitable desire to imitate what looks so easy. The results have proved, for the most part, to be flat and awkward, but these private efforts have prepared the way for a closer and more professional enquiry into, say, the Choruses of *Murder in the Cathedral.*

The consequent partial absorption of the Eliot idiom, coupled with the reading of some of the essays, has brought with it, frequently, a drastic remoulding of taste, an intolerant tidying up of the past. The effect is an astringent and exclusive one, and the Romantics suffer the most. If a sentence in a schoolboy essay begins 'Mr Eliot writes . . .', one recognizes at once the note of finality: no further discussion can be expected. Indeed, so sensitive and precise and final and strong are the essays that the schoolboy mind cannot meet them with rational argument, for the poet seems to have anticipated all possible lines of criticism. This is not a problem peculiar only to the young, but the meeting of a critical power, so thorough and so acute in those who may previously have known no other, is an experience that the resolute and highly intelligent alone can survive.

Again he has anticipated criticism:

> How unpleasant to meet Mr Eliot!

And if his writing or his conversation is 'so nicely'

> Restricted to What Precisely
> And If and Perhaps and But

'its purpose' (and here he is writing of complexity in writing) 'must be, first, the precise expression of finer shades of feeling and thought; second, the introduction of greater refinement and variety of music.'[1]

This is a turning-point, perhaps *the* turning-point, for the schoolboy. He will laugh pleasedly at the echoes of Edward Lear, delightedly at *The Book of Practical Cats*, whether there be echoes or not, and he can know in the prose and in the poetry the presence of high skill. If, from this point, he can begin to know—in spite of his proverbially irreverent attitude towards the great—the quality of the

[1] *What is a Classic?*, 1945.

mind that he is meeting, that he is in touch with someone whose life is dedicated to the portrayal of truth, then he can begin to grow towards maturity. If he can catch the sincerity of feeling in Eliot's works, then he can be led—to a gradually lessening extent—by the tactful guidance of his schoolmaster into a very wide field of discovery. For as soon as a young person begins to read Eliot humbly, but with courage, his capacity to feel and to understand is wonderfully refined. It would be absurd to make any exaggerated claims, and, in twenty years' experience of reading and talking about Eliot to schoolboys, comparatively few have been able to absorb at all deeply the more profound poems, and fewer still have continued to read him when they have left school.

The complexity, and what appears to the schoolboy to be an over-refinement, a sort of thinness in the poetry, prevent many from coming to the ever-deepening joy of the *Four Quartets*. Yet, in spite of this, an immense amount is achieved, if, from reading Eliot, a boy can have a dawning sense of the tradition of Christian culture in Europe, for this is none other than the possible field of discovery he can begin to make while at school. He can have this from attending a performance of *Murder in the Cathedral*—perhaps by acting in it—and he can be led to compare what he finds with 'the land of lobelias and tennis flannels'. Risks have to be taken, for it is salutary that the youth of the country should not be uncritical of the age in which it is growing-up. I was once reading some poems of Eliot and John Betjeman, interspersed with comment, to a group of Sixth-Form boys, and one of them came to me afterwards with the words 'Sir, you have described my parents exactly!' There was nothing but honesty in the remark. Yet the young and insecure do not take easily to satire, especially if it touches them directly. They like cosy things and they feel, at first anyhow, an absence of pity in the poetry of Eliot that they read, and it is only after a return to *Prufrock* that they do not laugh in the wrong places, and can sense the pathos and the sharp nerve of destiny that threads through the poem. But, as soon as that is caught in the tone and stress of the poetry, one can try to meet the desire to know the meaning of the lines and the background to individual poems. Boys are open to having their feelings touched, in spite of external evidence to the contrary, and it has been a distraction as fatal to an appreciation of 'La Figlia che Piange' to tell them that it was inspired by Eliot's disappointment at not seeing the 'Weeping Girl' statue in an Italian museum as the story of the man from Porlock has been to generations of schoolboy readers of 'Xanadu'.

The pictures of brittle, insensitive living are remorseless and clear, yet the balanced and, in the end, mature vision of Eliot's poetry must contain in the memory the lines

> I am moved by fancies that are curled
> Around the images, and cling:
> The notion of some infinitely gentle
> Infinitely suffering thing.

The young, if they are reminded, are always ready to see that there is this among the 'vacant lots' and the 'weeping multitudes', droop though they may. Indeed, they can scarcely believe in the reality of these scenes without it. And, in spite of itself, pity enters the seemingly barren poetry of *The Waste Land*, though the schoolboy but half understands the meaning.

The penetration into one poem will greatly help the understanding of another:

> What images return
> O my daughter

and need to be resolved

> Under sleep, where all the waters meet.

Here follows the deepening, and the growth of a habit of mind in the young to see and to see in, to see reflected in the face of time, on the one hand, boredom, on the other, eternity. One tends to think that the inner reality is more bearable to the young than to those already inflexibly set in their ways of thought, at least that they are less disturbed by silence than are their elders and that they are more open to a poetic experience. What happens to them in the middle years is not our business here.

In youth one's protections against reality are continually changing, and the best chance of a boy being able to deepen his understanding of such a reflective and analytical poet as Eliot is for him to try to understand what is happening to himself. He must know, for instance, something of the limitations of his own education. Where so much of his teaching is directed towards clarifying the material presented to him, he must be shown that there is a vast area of knowledge of which he can say that he knows but does not know the reality. It is, in truth, the fear of the mystery implied in his kind of knowing that frightens so many people into a state of closed and dogged activism.

To have been brought up with Eliot and not to have penetrated beyond his own critical attitude to society has, in my experience, induced a thin and derisive attitude of mind. The mockery in this turns, not only against society, but it turns inwardly against the individual himself who knows that there is more to discover in the poetry, but knows, too, that he, for one reason or another, cannot find it. The task, then, of the person presenting Eliot's poetry to the young is to let the poetry speak for itself in the best possible way, but this has to be supported by guidance in knowing what kind of meaning to look for in it. I knew a boy who, after meeting *The Waste Land* for the first time, bought a book on the Tarot pack of cards, and another who, with greater profit, took the poet's advice and read Jessie Weston's *From Ritual to Romance.* A search into the sources of the poetry cannot be followed far by a schoolboy, but even a few discoveries bring him confidence and show him how the transforming mind of the poet has worked; it may also bring closer together a study of the essays and of the poetry.

Meaning radiates from reality, and it is for the one who has seen much of reality to expand the capacity of those who have not seen, and then, in turn, to learn to see more deeply from those that he teaches. Thus the richness of meaning can be shared by a group of boys ready to dwell reflectively on a single line that they are likely to have read many times *un*reflectively.

> They know and do not know, that acting is suffering
> And suffering is action.

Through a series of meanings of the verb 'to act' one can arrive at a deeper understanding of the pain that is felt by a person who is acting a part in life and not being himself. . . . Thence to a meditation on the wholeness of the act of love that martyrdom entails and the pain of preparation in being able to accept the decision to be a martyr. . . . And so to a deeper realization of the enfolding Love of God that entirely possesses a person called to martyrdom. To write this in three short sentences makes the movement of the meditation sound neat and cold-blooded, whereas it is, for the most part, slow and hesitant. Not everything is understood. Lines dwell in the mind for many days so that one cannot remember when they were not there. Thus the poetry is allowed to speak for itself and the meaning to dawn upon one. 'It must have been very difficult for Thomas *not* to have been a martyr' was a remark made by a boy who had understood much of the meaning of the play.

Popular prophecy would perhaps claim that modern youth cannot be brought to think about martyrdom, that all his pursuits represent a flight from such a thing, whereas there have never been more possible deaths that a man may die, and these have not ceased to be interesting, at least to the young. It remains true that the Christian faith alone can make something positive out of the suffering of life. To understand this deeply is the work of a life-time, and the movement towards understanding it brings one inevitably to a meditation on the relationship between birth and dying, in the sense that one is, in the Christian teaching, reborn spiritually even as one dies to oneself in this life.

With an eye to the future, and with thoughts on the wide range of reading that may, in future years, accompany the *Four Quartets*, it has been helpful I have discovered to read aloud extracts from Walter Hilton's *The Scale of Perfection*. The risk must be taken that some will be out of their depths, and, in my experience, it may be taken so long as one stresses the sense of the present and its continuity with the past. 'That which hath been is now . . .' is written in the *Book of Ecclesiastes*.

Thus through early preparation at school, in times of freedom from the modern toil of exams, a few have gathered the strength of interest to sustain them in a future study of the poetry of T. S. Eliot. And, of those few, many have written in gratitude of the poet.

Teaching the *Four Quartets* to Schoolgirls

ELIZABETH HAMILTON

'I OFTEN think it's a pity that there is only one great poet in our time—T. S. Eliot. I wish that there were some others so that one could choose.' This was said to me by a girl of eighteen, although I have heard the same sentiment expressed by others. It is significant that in the whole of this school section only two other names occur—those of Betjeman and Dylan Thomas. Yet, there again, perhaps the one glorious feature that Eliot, Betjeman and Thomas all hold in common is that they are all gloriously independent poets; they have had their imitators (and parody can often be the highest form of flattery), yet none of them has appeared as a poet of a 'group' or 'movement'.

My experience of teaching Eliot has been confined principally to the *Four Quartets*, and I have been surprised, in view of the abstruse nature of the thought behind the poems, how many girls have quickly been able to make them their own. Some find a simple pleasure in the lyrical passages—are charmed by the sound of the words, caught by the primary and primeval power of the poetry, which is the power of incantation. In some respects this pleasure may be compared to that of a person who, knowing no Greek, delights to listen to a chorus of Euripides, or, with little knowledge of French, to a poem of Baudelaire. In the section that follows, one girl (Jane Westwood on page 116), writing of Eliot's characters in his plays, says that they 'belong to no century' and that they appear to exist in 'a kind of lost limbo'. The truth is that the stories of Greek drama are so powerful and primary that we do not have to know them consciously for them to be consciously present with us all the time.

I remember the shock of pleasure of a pupil who discovered that Sir Henry Harcourt-Reilly is a reincarnation of Heracles in Euripides's *Alcestis*.[1] A pleasure of a somewhat similar nature was experienced by another who, on accidentally discovering who Krishna was, found her mind flashing back to *The Dry Salvages*.

It is more than probable that a girl will find herself hard put to explain such lines as:

> Who then devised the torment? Love.
> Love is the unfamiliar Name
> Behind the hands that wove
> The intolerable shirt of flame.

Or she may wonder why:

> The houses are all gone under the sea

and:

> The dancers are all gone under the hill.

Yet her puzzlement will not detract from her pleasure in the poetry itself. Her first response must be intuitive. Later reason can be brought to bear upon the poem's theme and argument. For poetry, as mysterious as love, speaks to the soul through the senses—a fact which explains why the intuitive pupil will suddenly grasp a meaning, whereas her more academic or scholarly rival will still be groping in the dark. The names King Lear and Edward Lear are easily associated; they may come together as a result of a slip of the tongue, or the ravings on the heath may genuinely summon up early nursery nonsense verse. Ultimately, the way of approach is immaterial, yet once established, as Mary Drummond shows on page 105, it offers a valuable double context in which to see Eliot the nonsense poet as well as Eliot the poet of the *Four Quartets*.

I have only taught one of the girls represented in this book, although several of my pupils submitted entries. Again, some of the girls represented here pinned notes on their manuscripts to the effect

[1] A colleague of mine, reading the piece on page 115 by Wendy Carver, thinks a similar shock of pleasure may await this child if she discovers in Harcourt-Reilly's advice, 'Go in peace and work out your salvation diligently', an echo from Buddhistic teaching.

that they had never been taught any Eliot as part of their English curriculum. Again, some of the pieces selected for inclusion were submitted not because those who taught the children considered them good, but because the rest of the class insisted that they should be sent in and so given a chance. This reminds me that one has to be careful not to apply too much reason and logic when reading the Quartets in class—at least at the beginning. To break apart the delicate structure in which a poet has concealed his message by too much analysis can be a barbarous and disastrous act. A child's spontaneous delight in poetry may be extinguished—sometimes for a term or so, sometimes for ever. A poem should be allowed, in the first instance, to make its own impact. Question and probing can follow later. One would do well to take to heart the words of the poet himself:

> I said to my soul, be still, and let the dark come upon you
> Which shall be the darkness of God.

The reflective, unemotional quality of much of Eliot's writing is satisfying to those of a mathematical or scientific bent who are sometimes inclined to disclaim interest in poetry. His meditations on time, though based on a concept as old as *Ecclesiastes*, are in tune with minds brought up on relativity:

> Time present and time past
> Are both perhaps present in time future,
> And time future contained in time past.

I remember his presentation of the Incarnation being described in a girl's essay as a 'geometrical presentation of the truth'. She was referring to:

> The point of intersection of the timeless
> With time.

The intellectual core of Eliot's work has been said to appeal more to men than women. Whether this is true I do not know, but it certainly has an appeal among girls. It is a challenge to which an alert mind is quick to respond. His message, too, with its emphasis on darkness and deprivation of spirit, is also a challenge, though one which may deter the less courageous in spirit. Yet his teaching is positive, his darkness, which is the darkness of St John of the Cross, is full of light, and ringing through the darkness comes the reiterated message of Dame Julian of Norwich:

> And all shall be well and
> All manner of thing shall be well.

The poet of the *Four Quartets* has moved a long way from the poet of *The Waste Land* and *The Hollow Men*. The latter poems expressed, in a manner perfect after its kind, the disillusionment of a disillusioned age. The *Four Quartets*, on the other hand, are an expression of hope and love. Behind the Nessus shirt of torment there is love. The world today stands in need of love; speaks of it in political assemblies, preaches of it from pulpits. To a new generation—one from which tomorrow's critics will come—Eliot, who had seemed to an earlier age the poet of cynicism, has become the poet of love.

A Garland from the Young

INTRODUCTION

WHEN Mr Braybrooke asked me to add a laurel leaf to Mr Eliot's crown I thought I had plenty to offer, and indeed I had; but when I came to study them I found them wanting in one way or another, they were of uneven growth, lopsided, or they struck me as having been picked, too obviously, from other writers' gardens. All sorts of comments I could make, but together they did not form a coherent whole; while some of them were so contradictory that no resort to paradox could reconcile them—as, for example, that though in Mr Eliot's work the words are plain, each carefully chosen and embedded in its setting like a jewel, his general drift is sometimes obscure and subject to several interpretations. Again, he is a traditionalist and an innovator—his roots in the past, his flowers and branches in a present that not long ago was a future. It was these two elements in him, the stationary and the moving, that most worried me, for though it was easy to see the distance traversed between, for example, the Prufrock poems and the *Four Quartets*, it was much less easy to convey it in a sentence that should have the shapeliness of the laurel leaf I had in mind yet could not bring to maturity. Nor could I find a metaphor to help me. A signpost pointing to a path hardly trodden as yet? No, for Mr Eliot, the signpost also moves. A satisfactory synthesis eluded me. Mr Eliot's work remained not inchoate but disparate, and what use is a shredded laurel leaf, except as an old collector's device for putting to sleep moths and butterflies?

Out of the mouths of babes and sucklings. . . . Mr Eliot himself had told me of the interest that school-children in America take in his work, and quite independently of this, the Editor of this 'Celebration' had the idea of asking school-children in England to add their garland to the birthday fête. So he sent me his selection of the best contributions and asked me to sponsor them.

The ages of the contributors range from fourteen to eighteen. Several things struck me: one was that more girls than boys had written about Mr Eliot. Why? I asked myself. I am no authority on adolescence, but I have always believed that the literary instinct was more precocious and more widespread among boys than girls. And I should have guessed that two outstanding qualities of Mr Eliot's work, the intellectual and the religious, were more likely to appeal to boys than girls. A personal element there is: besides his own personality, there are characters who appear in Mr Eliot's poems, as well as the *dramatis personae* of his plays: Sweeney, Burbank with his Baedeker, Bleistein with his cigar, Princess Volupine, Miss Helen Slingsby. But they are all treated with irony or satire as warnings, examples to be avoided; whereas girls are, or used to be, passionately interested in people for their own sake and impatient of any attitude or theory which makes abstractions of them. The 'gossipy' element so dear to Daisy Ashford (and Jane Austen) is almost absent from Mr Eliot's work. His people may be real people, but they are usually also illustrations of some tendency. Yet of the original contributors (from whom those represented here have been seeded) the girls outnumber the boys by roughly three to one.

More surprising still is the predominantly analytical character of the essays. It often happens that both boys and girls are gifted with a creative imagination that (in most cases) does not outlast their adolescence; but the critical faculty—intuition and insight plus the ability to express them—is, I should have thought, very rare. Yet here we find it, and the power not only to isolate ideas but to make illuminating and sometimes challenging comparisons, and to interpret symbols. At these children's age I would not have made head or tail of Mr Eliot (I cannot always now), and I am astonished at the understanding they possess, the breadth, length and depth of the vision unfolded to their innocent eyes. Does it mean that Mr Eliot's thought and the manner of its expression have passed into the language? Have these boys and girls had better teachers than I had? Or are they simply more intelligent?

On this note of modesty, which is anything but false, I will stop, and let the youngsters speak for themselves. L. P. HARTLEY

The Wedding of Daphnis

Δάφνιδος Ἀργείου νύμφας τε γάμῳ Γαλατείας
τέρποντες κορυδοὶ καὶ ἀκανθίδες ὕμνον ἄειδον
δώνακι Πᾶνος ἴσον· θαλεροὶ δὲ χορον σατυρίσκοι
ἀρτίζοντο; περιπλίκτους πόδας ἐγκροτέοντες.
τᾶμος ἄρα δρύσιν ὑψιτέραις αἴγειρος ἐρίσδει
φύλλα καλὰ κροτεουσ᾽ ὡς κύμβαλα δεινὰ Κυβηβης.
ἦνθον καὶ τρόμεροι πτῶκες πολίαι τε χιμάιραι.
Νυμφαι κασταλίδες προς τοῖς κατέβασαν ἀπ ᾽οὔρους
ταῖσι κόμαις αἱ μὲν στεφάνους κροκόεντας ἔχοισαι
αἱ δ᾽ἐνὶ χέρσὶ μάκρους θύρσους ἀπαλαῖσι φέροισαι
καὶ Ζέφυροι ψοφέοντες ἐνὶ πτελέων πετάλοισι
ὡς ψιθυρίσδοντες θαλάμους δοκέουσιν ἐπαινεῖν.
καὶ μὰν αἶγας ἄγων ἐπιχειρεῖ Ἀμύντιχος ᾄδειν
προς ῾ρεέθρον, φωνῇ παραμούσῳ καὶ μάλ᾽ ἐουσῇ.
ἀλλ᾽ὦ, Πιερίδες, μὴ λήγετε Δάφνιδι κλεινῷ
καὶ νὺ χαριζόμεναι ὡς νύμφαν θελξῇ ἀοιδαῖς.
"*῾Υμὴν*, ὦ *Υμεναῖε*, γάμῳ ἐπὶ τῷδε χαρείης."

All the birds of Argos sang for joy at the wedding of Daphnis and Galatea, the crested lark and the goldfinch, like the cross-flute or shepherd's pipe. And Satyrs set to dancing, making the earth shake beneath their criss-crossing feet. And poplars vied with shaggy oaks in shaking their leaves like cymbals of the Idaean mother. Flocks of kids and shy hares came to the marriage; after them came nymphs down from the mountains, some with garlands of yellow crocuses in their hair, and others carrying ivy-wreathed thyrses in their hands. Even the Zephyrs rustling the ivy on the elm trees, just as when they gently disturb the blue water, seemed to whisper a marriage song, as though in approval of the wedding. Little Amyntas leading his flock of goats tried to sing their praise, although his voice was far from musical.

Pierian maidens! do not cease to favour glorious Daphnis, that,
by his songs, he may delight his bride!
'Oh, Hymen, God of weddings, look with favour at this marriage!'

PIERS CROKE (AGE 17)

On Thomas Stearns Eliot

Sometimes in his quite inexplicable ecstasy of sound T. S. Eliot produces what can only be called noises. They express animal feeling of beauty or disgust. They symbolize all the pain in sound or joy produced since primitive creation—but yet, are only noises:

Weialala leia
Wallala leialala.

And yet it is 'Music [that] crept by me upon the waters'; strange ears, then, that transform animal sounds to passing music. Mad, perhaps? I think not. In his poems are incorporated two persons—separated in literature by all the wealth of centuries rich in a harvest of rhythm and poetry; two persons—one real, one fictitious—one mad, one sane, both with the same name—Lear.

'How pleasant to know Mr Lear', writes Edward Lear, conceitedly, but the same is true of Mr Eliot, 'Who has written such volumes of stuff'—equally true of both; but there the likeness—in personal appearance anyway—ends.

But, and here I produce as evidence two choruses, their works run as two railway lines, gleaming silver—touching, interchanging and swinging away to continue apart. See and compare:

D was a Duck,
With spots on his back,
Who lived in the water,
And always said Quack!

Childish indeed, but—

Here we go round the prickly pear,
Prickly pear, prickly pear;
Here we go round the prickly pear
At five o'clock in the morning,

is childish also, a child's game twisted and contorted into harsh, aimless disillusionment.

There are likenesses, blatant and obvious, but these similarities are only as like as a stream, rippling and lapping on pebbles, shallow and bubbling, is like the grey swirling masses of the ocean, tossed and distorted in strange waves by invisible and most potential forces.

Edward Lear's is meaningless chatter, the babble of a ceaseless stream; Eliot's is the intangible power of the sea, sweeping all before it, forceful in its mighty depths.

But there is the other Lear—King Lear—who raves upon the heath with an old man's frenzy; the sound of his voice is as the breakers on the cliffs destroying themselves in their own life:

> And thou, all-shaking thunder,
> Strike flat the thick rotundity o' the world

he shrieks in his madness. And how like to

> Thunder rolled by the rolling stars,
> Simulates triumphal cars . . .
> Hunt the heavens and the plain
> Whirled in a vortex.

The king has majesty; T. S. Eliot has power, not over the thunder but over language. It rolls with the thunder; it, too, simulates triumph; it is power—the power of childhood and madness; of a king and a joker; of majesty and freedom, an invisible and intangible power. But the under-current of this torrent is destroying and killing, meaning Death, as his disillusionment falls as a heavy stone, crushing his work:

> Between the idea
> And the reality
> Between the motion
> And the act
> Falls the Shadow.

MARY DRUMMOND (AGE 14)

'In My Beginning is My End'

When one can truthfully claim to understand the first line of *East Coker*, it might almost be said that one is in a position to understand Mr Eliot. The very absurdity of this would then strike one, the natural reaction being to doubt one's former comprehension of the statement.

If a man gazing out of a window claims to understand the sky, be he expert astronomer or merely a casual observer, it does not occur to us to take him seriously. Behind what the eye can see lies the entire vault of the solar system which—we are told—despite its intricate and innumerable conjunctions of whirling planets, burning stars and icy, revolving moons, fills but a fraction of that infinite, intangible mystery of—space. Who, therefore, with even the insufficient knowledge man has gained of what lies beyond the azure arches of the heavens, can claim to know the skies? And who, to know, to understand, Mr Eliot? For with the sky he has height and depths inestimable, and beyond that which the eye can perceive, what breadth, what volume, what immeasurable space of thought does his poetry cover.

We do not, then, understand the depths of his poetry, but can, however, perceive the surface of meaning in a work which, to our great-grandfathers, would have been incomprehensible. In the same way that we now appreciate the French impressionists whose work was half a century before their time, we can appreciate what in Mr Eliot would have seemed to our ancestors a crime. It is because, although we may not understand in its full realization what his poetry means, it is the expression of an age, of our age. In him we see ourselves. We see the disillusionment, the depression of modern life. When the idle rich of the Nineteenth Century saw Renoir, Dégas and Cezanne as stark, unimaginative and crude, they did not realize that they were seeing a reflection of what, in fact, the world of their children and grandchildren was to be like. And as did Cezanne and Dégas, Mr Eliot has captured and portrayed, not only what men see with their eyes, but what they experience in their hearts.

Although many of us, even today, find Mr Eliot's poetry difficult, it is because of this reason. We are a people who shut our eyes to the facts, we see only the deceptive blue of the sky, and should we traverse as far as the solar system, we do not venture within the measureless bounds of space.

'*Here we go round the prickly pear . . .*' Eaten up with those all-important money matters, we have become ensnared within the revolving circle of ambition, power, atoms and the harnessing of nature to become man's weapon to destroy man. We are caught up in it and whirled round as surely as if we were trapped in one of our own made, labour-saving devices, the washing machine. And yet we are too busy in our daily routine of watching machines of our creation churning out creationless knowledge to realize that it is ourselves, in our struggle for power—the power to destroy—that we can see in Mr Eliot's poetry, bumping our noses as futilely as a goldfish in a glass bowl, '*Here we go round the prickly pear*'.

Mr Eliot is all of the extraordinary combination of paradox and antitheses that goes to make up the Twentieth Century. His poetry can, if we will let it, really mean something. It is great because it is true, we are 'the hollow men' and 'life is very long', but, above all, we must realize that '*Thine is the kingdom*' and that the systems, the icy stars and burning moons are the product—even as we are—of a great creation. From Mr Eliot we can grasp that there is something more infinite than eternal television; that nuclear power did not form of itself; that the world will not end in a 'whimper' for 'In my end is my beginning'.

FRANCESCA TOLHURST (AGE 14)

A Contrast of Landscapes: *'Virginia' and 'Usk'*

'Virginia' and 'Usk' are the difference between death and life. 'Virginia' personifies eternity, while 'Usk' portrays only the ephemeral beauty of peace and imagination.

For the person who walks and gazes in that region, imagination conjures up the knight with the lance and the elusive white hart, but, with the same breath, forbids him to resurrect the past, to 'let them sleep' because he could 'gently dip, but not too deep' into 'old enchantments'. The 'Usk' is old but not eternal.

'Virginia' waits, waits through all eternity. The repetition of 'wait', the length of 'Red river, river, river', and the heavy stillness portrayed by the whole poem gives an added impression of patient, hopeless waiting which will last till 'the end of the endless journey to no end'.

The lines

> No will is still as a river
> Still

reinforce this impression to such an extent that one feels the burden is so weighty that it is almost crushing.

Though the poet says in 'Virginia' that the trees are

> Living, living,
> Never moving

the whole impression brings out the lifelessness in the landscape and the decay. The trees are purple, or white, without the life of the green leaves. The river flows silently, redly, without moving the heat, and without noise, instead of splashing noisily, and raising white manes on galloping green waves. 'Gates wait', and are never touched. The silence is stirred only by

> the mocking-bird
> Heard once.

Even the long words, the repeated r's and the monotonous rhythm bring out this keynote of the poem, whereas, in 'Usk', life bounds through the shorter, quicker, more irregular rhythm. Instead of the heavy, still heat, there is 'grey light', with visions of a cold wind beyond it, and 'green air', and green is a natural and soothing colour. Instead of blank trees, a white hart appears behind a well, and while nothing moves in 'Virginia', in 'Usk' roads dip and roads rise, finding 'the hermit's chapel, the pilgrim's prayer'.

It could be thought that the only two movements in the poems would resemble each other, but even these are in complete contrast to each other. The mocking bird trills, once, immediately bringing out the silence, loneliness and ugliness of the landscape. The branch is broken, and the harsh sound breaks the peace of the scene.

Even the thoughts inspired by these landscapes seem to come from different words, 'iron thoughts' from the Hades that is 'Virginia', for it is the land of the dead that live eternally. Thoughts invincible, eternal, blank, yet still present like the metal, and just as dead as it after numberless centuries have weighed upon it, is the only burden that the 'red river' carries. 'Where the roads dip and where roads rise' come thoughts of living creatures, of 'the white hart behind the well', of the noble knight leaning down to take the lance from the groom beside him, of 'old enchantments', and because true life comes only from God, in the hermit's thoughts, 'the pilgrim's prayer', only where they are can life be.

DIANA STEWARD (AGE 14)

Musical Form and Preludes

It is notable that *The Waste Land* and *Four Quartets*—meditations upon the nature of life or experience rather than trains of thought concerning particular experiences—should both use the highly stylized Quartet form. This is in itself similar to a strict musical form within which patterning and control of imagery and rhythm are handled as a composer would his instruments, phrases and emphases. The value of this technique of composition, which has fascinated T. S. Eliot, has been commented on by many critics; it is certainly the means whereby those poems which use it fulfil Eliot's dictum, that 'true poetry can communicate before it is understood'.

I believe that the first time we know Eliot to have experimented with writing poetry in something akin to a musical form is in the poem called *Preludes* from his earliest volume. An examination of the poem will show how far the poetic pleasure of reading it lies in the quasi-musical technique by which imagery and rhythm are used within the musical form of a sequence of preludes. I also believe that there is a significance consistent with Eliot's later poetic interest in the use of such a musical form in this particular poem.

Very different, of course, from the Quartet form, these four preludes are a little suite, with conclusion, of poetic variations upon a mood. The chiasmic subject arrangement is the most obvious feature: Morning, Evening, Evening, Morning. This provides a simple delight, which should not be scorned, in the form for its own sake. In addition, it emphasizes the attitude of the poem, portraying the dreary cycle in which evening is simply a prelude to night, night to morning and another day, and day to evening and another night again. Against this pattern plays the poet's use of images. In the first two preludes they suggest weariness on a physical plane—the smells, the dreary streets and houses, the shabby-looking people. The third and fourth preludes are concerned with another plane of experience: the sordid images of the trampled soul. This, then, is no mere 'imagist' poem; the imagery itself plays a counterpart to the chiasmus that we have already observed.

The 'conclusion' (which I take to be the last seven lines) again shows Eliot's concern for the arrangement of the units of his poetry as well as the care for felicity of expression within those units. After the insistently dreary picture of the four preludes comes a moment of strange illumination. These four lines express a feeling quite different from that of the physical or mental imagery of the preludes: a suggestion of something ethereal yet more sweetly and intensely real than what has gone before. This is achieved by the use of words of a different, because of an abstract, quality not belonging to the dreariness of humanity—'some infinitely gently / Infinitely suffering thing'. Then, with a return to the original theme, crashes the final chord of misery. The repetition of 'vacant lots' is used for added vigour, for it comes charged with associations of its first context—a device that the poet uses with increasing skill.

What has been separated in analysis into various elements is read, not by an act of synthesis, but as one substance. The poet's thought formed the patterns, and the patterns gave direction to his thoughts to bring the unity of the finished poem. That one substance is a criticism of life. Although limited to town life, *Preludes* has an air of universality not apparent in the more particular conception and observation of *The Love Song of J. Alfred Prufrock* and of the other poems in that Prufrock volume. This is what makes the strict ordering of *Preludes*, in a way similar to musical composition, so significant. *The Waste Land* and *Four Quartets* are also criticisms of life from a universal point of view, and also have (with far greater development) this musically ordered composition. Further, in *Four Quartets*, the Quartet form reaches its perfection in the same poetic experience in which T. S. Eliot expresses the spiritual peace of which he shows an awareness in the '*Datta, Dayadhvam, Damyata*' of *The Waste*

Land. But this awareness is hesitantly shown in Eliot's earlier, smaller, but poetically successful attempt at a patterned interpretation of experience, which we perceive in *Preludes.*

JOHN NICHOLSON (AGE 17)

The Voice of T. S. Eliot

Mr Eliot, the critic, says, 'the progress of an artist is a . . . continual extinction of personality'. Yet in reading his own criticism it is as if we were reading something we had not been invited to read (and yet Mr Eliot hoped we would).

If I offered some of my own work to Mr E. M. Forster to criticize, he would be honest yet kind. If he was not satisfied with what I had written, I would feel ashamed that I had been satisfied myself. But, had Mr Eliot not approved, I would immediately want to defend it, feeling he was wrong. His manner would alienate me, though I knew really that his authority was perhaps greater than Mr Forster's.

And yet, when we forget his voice it seems bold to be critical. What Mr Eliot says is wise. The piercingness of his words and sentences make their mark on our minds. He makes one work. One must attend. We cannot read the end of the sentence and the phrase before and understand the sentence as a whole. But as we wander off on a branching track, there it is again; he does not catch us back with a friendly grasp of the hand as Mr Forster does, but with a call over his shoulder so that we come guiltily back and follow him again. He uses continually the condescending, assured: 'of course', 'one would suppose', 'Tares to which we are all subject', but we feel he does not think *he* is subject to them. We are glad to be accounted on his side. He is so clever. We are so inferior. We stretch our minds as far as possible. He has us in his grasp when we actually read his work. But away, we say he judges:

> As if he were a god to punish
> Not a man of their [the author's] infirmity.

The same voice is there in the poetry, yet it is not so oppressive; because the personal feeling is not acceptable in work concerning other men, whereas in poetry it is. In the underground train:

> And you see behind every face the mental emptiness deepen
> Leaving only the growing terror of nothing to think about.

Yet we feel that he had plenty to think about. We are on his side of the train, then, looking at those on the opposite seat. But on the next journey, away from him, we would be on the other seat, with Mr Eliot alone on the first.

The confidence is still there. He has a complete grip on all the verse, what he is saying, the allusions. But he is more intent on his aim, less concerned with us. We do not throw it back in his face when he says:

> the only wisdom we can hope to acquire
> Is the wisdom of humility: humility is endless.

Yet this voice has the power to express feelings, atmosphere, moments, moods so that they are touchable, tastable. Behind all the poetry it is his voice that gives a kind of tangible thickness to everything. It is impersonal, at the back of the mind, accusing, sad, wondering, yet confident, continuous. It is most obvious in the plays. It is behind the atmosphere of *The Family Reunion*: darkness, a big house, wondering, showing off, questions, muddle. Somehow we feel safer with it.

We feel sick in the Sweeney poems: 'She yawns and draws a stocking up'. It is sordid. Mr. Eliot gets the mood in a line. The 'feels' in the earlier works, especially the plays, are tougher than in the *Four Quartets*. We can touch them too easily. They are too thick. It is the same with a symbol like: 'our brains unskinned like the layers of an onion'. But the feeling is never completely sordid; there is a hint of a remembrance of beauty, too. The drunken 'goonights' of Lil and Albert end with Ophelia's heart-broken good nights.

It is when Mr Eliot is describing something naturally fresh, like a child of nature, that the rising feeling of excitement comes in one. He must have felt those moments himself, whereas one suspected the old sordidness of *The Waste Land* or Sweeney had not been felt through and through. But: 'An old white horse galloped away in the meadow.' And we get that moment of joy.

A.S.—8

The day I lost my butterfly net,
I remember the silence and the hushed excitement.

The treble voices on the lawn.

It is when he has really felt that we are hit. The *Four Quartets* are better than the earlier works: nature is something sincere and pure in them. We feel that intangible excitement with: 'the children in the leaves' and 'Quick, said the bird, find them, find them'.

ELIZABETH GORDON (AGE 18)

Why do I like T. S. Eliot? The thought has often passed through my mind. I have said to myself that I like him because of his way of writing or his delightful fictitious names. But I always end up with the same reason. This is, I never get tired of reading his work—and each time I read it, the more I understand it. For instance, I can read one of his poems through once, or even twice, and perhaps get a story or line of events out of it. But on the third and fourth readings I find some definite message or moral in it. If possible, I think that it is better if you can get someone to read it to you the first two times. Then read it through yourself. One of the best renderings I have ever heard was that given by the late Dylan Thomas.

. . . The last remark I am going to make is probably the most important—that I find T. S. Eliot so completely relaxing, especially when worried or bothered. A poem which really does relax me is *Animula*. It seems to unroll itself like a carpet. I can imagine myself to be there, moving among the legs and tables of the chairs. It takes no effort to read, which is pleasing in this world of noise with its 'sounds of horns and motors'. TIMOTHY BRINDLEY (AGE 14)

Mr Eliot is like a drug, intoxicating but dangerous. In one line he can distort one's life; in two, he can sink one into the deepest depths of depression, and in three, he can transform the world. . . . His poetry can be compared with champagne which can bring one to the highest, most blissful happiness, or the unhappiest, most morose and miserable melancholia. Yet one can look through the champagne and see the window the other side. One can read Mr Eliot's poetry, but not the man on the other side.

MARGARET WAUGH (AGE 14)

Some of his poems are as subtle as snakes, with small destructive tongues, darting hither and thither, giving fleeting impressions of some deeper meaning in the background, causing a great, and seemingly unquenchable, thirst for more, yet satisfying as they do so.

SHAN HAILEY (AGE 14)

In a time when the peace of nations is being kept paradoxically by a deadlock of fear, to read Mr Eliot's work is to find a clue to individual peace in the enlightenment of one civilized mind. Like the late Gilbert Murray, Mr Eliot is essentially civilized; there is nothing crude in his work. . . . Where so many of our modern dramatist's storm away into depths of despair, and see through squalor and corruption only more sordid misery, unable in their righteous anger (I prefer to call it immature shortsightedness) to find any hint of untainted beauty, and giving their subjects a brutal, exaggerated treatment which distorts so-called realism and leaves only a sense of frustration, Mr Eliot can treat similar subjects acting beside these modern 'Job's comforters' as a skilled physician. Very few dramatists can, after knocking the whole social system for six, restore self-confidence so miraculously, so that you leave the theatre with the knowledge that your salvation to a great extent lies in yourself: in the words of that amazing Eliot creation, Sir Henry Harcourt-Reilly: 'Go in peace and work out your salvation diligently.'

We see Celia Coplestone in *The Cocktail Party* and Harry in *The Family Reunion* preparing to embark on a new way of living, both content to live with their own inadequate selves: her way leads through martyrdom to triumph; his is to carry his own existence when his crime has been expiated. Lavinia and Edward Chamberlayne are a different matter: they have to solve the problem so often used by Ionesco—that of being unable to communicate with each other. Yet Mr Eliot leaves one with the belief that they, too, will succeed.

WENDY CARVER (AGE 15)

T. S. Eliot's poetry affects me keenly, and in a completely different manner from anything I have ever known, because it is literally honest to God.

PENELOPE HODGES (AGE 15: 'I have never been taught any Eliot')

Mr Eliot has re-vitalized the poetic vocabulary; he has abandoned rhyme, since its inevitability destroys its effect, and uses it only for an unsuspected effect.

GEORGE KENYON (AGE 17)

When I had finished reading *The Hollow Men* I could hardly bear to go on reading. Life is not empty and dull like that. There must be some theme or purpose behind it all, otherwise why are we here? *The Waste Land* made me think as no other poem has done.

MARY HOWELL (AGE 17: 'I have never had lessons on Eliot, or read any critical essays concerning his work')

T. S. Eliot understands our questions and can judge the delicate balance of human relationships. He is to us what Agatha was to Harry, Reilly to Celia, and his conscience to Thomas Becket. He presents our case, but finally leaves us to make our own decision.

JUDITH SCOTT (AGE 17)

All T. S. Eliot's four plays have particular things in common. It came as a shock to realize that *The Cocktail Party* was being acted in a modern setting and modern costume. Then I understood I had always thought of the plays as situated in a kind of universal limbo. The characters belong to no definite century, but are set to resolving certain problems which might happen in any time. Also, the plays all seem to end in a beginning. The problem set, to impose an order on life, is solved. A system of relationships with life, with others, with self, and in *Murder in the Cathedral* with God, has been established. From there, the plays look onward.

JANE WESTWOOD (AGE 17)

He has the knowledge of his own limitations. He knows that 'the culture of the individual cannot be isolated from that of the group', and says so plainly in his *Notes Towards the Definition of Culture.* He therefore gives his culture to the world, and with it gives a portrait of the world as it is. May it take notice of itself.

ANITA SIMMONS (AGE 17)

I approached *The Waste Land* as one who had heard much of it, but knew nothing about it. . . . I should also add that before I read *The Waste Land* I knew nothing of modern poetry and secretly abhorred it because I thought it was deliberately 'high-brow'. In short, to me, modern poetry was not poetry at all.

The first thing therefore that pleased me about this poem was that it *was* poetry, and that though it might be obscure, nevertheless, being 'genuine poetry', it 'communicated before it was understood'. I spotted countless references to Shakespeare and the Bible which impressed me because they reminded me of Browning—the only poet I had ever seriously studied before. Again I was impressed by the poem's realism, which reminded me of Orwell's *Nineteen Eighty-Four*:

> Flushed and decided, he assaults at once;
> Exploring hands encounter no defence.

Finally, I liked, but did not understand, the interpolations in foreign tongues—Latin, French, Italian, German and Greek. It is hard to explain why I liked these unfamiliar quotations, but perhaps it was because they added a professional touch, and, too, we all secretly pride ourselves on our pronunciation of foreign words: '*Le Prince d'Aquitaine à la tour abolie.*' Or, which is simpler: 'Shantih shantih shantih.'

JEREMY JACKSON (AGE 17)

I revolt from Eliot's view of society in *The Waste Land.* He believes that there is no life, no virility in it; there is no passion, values have become debased; love is a sexual act in which the female is indifferent, the male lustful. . . . The poem is the symbol of an age of decadent artists. Perhaps John Osborne's *The Entertainer* marks a turning point in the direction of a more sympathetic, less critical view of the individual within society. The need today is for construction and not destruction, for giving and not taking, for unselfishness and work. I only hope that the intellectual temper of England will in twenty years time be such that *The Waste Land* and in another field action painting will be regarded as examples of decadent thought.

MICHAEL PIPER (AGE 18)

It has been said of Homer that he wrote of ordinary things in an extraordinary way; the same is true of Mr Eliot. . . . His highly condensed ideas create a chain-reaction in poetry.

BARBARA PINDELSKA (AGE 18)

T. S. Eliot as a Classical Scholar

W. F. JACKSON KNIGHT

'THERE is no interrogation in his eyes'—a perfect example, not really of 'marquetry',[1] but of the classical poet's correct behaviour for channelling a charge which the dead poets of the tradition have stored. 'Thou hast no speculation in those eyes'—the eyes of the ghost in *Macbeth*; but this time, in these other eyes, there is speculation, that is, sight; speculation, yes, but not interrogation. To apprehend the dynamics of this substitution no keyed-up critical power is needed. A loosely-straying fancy is enough. The Coriolanian leader of 'Triumphal March' is detached, like and not like a ghost, for he is in this world but not of it. Perhaps all poets hail the superhuman, or seek it, appraise it, trust and mistrust it—and more consciously if they are aware through scholarship of the finer tempering in words.

The ghost does not see. The conqueror sees, and his eyes are 'watchful, waiting, perceiving, indifferent', with no need to interrogate, enjoying a loneliness of life rather than of death. He is more human than others, not, like Banquo's ghost, less. The problem, then, in the poem is well put. It goes beyond previous statements as it should; the setting has, as it should have, the posited modern 'sordor'; and images provided with help from Shakespeare and dozens more, images of power in a moving mythology, give the solution in correct emotional terms. It is the way the ancients, Greek and Roman, but not only Greek and Roman, made their poetry.

This canalization of tradition to generate charges of meaning

[1] E. K. Brown, 'Mr Eliot and some Enemies', *University of Toronto Quarterly*, October 1938, p. 81, citing Elizabeth Atkins; cf. A. J. Creedy, 'Eliot and the Classics', *Orpheus*, Catania, I, January 1954, pp. 42–58, an article which goes deeper than mine and should be read with it, especially for Eliot's organic and pervasive use of classical derivations and the basic importance to him of Greek philosophy.

probably happens in the minds of nearly all poets, and it can happen in the minds of people who are not poets unless, by acting so, they become poetic. But when it is as precise, economical and challenging as this, and in particular when it so strikes fire by a sharp and minute contrast-in-similarity, any supposition that all this was done without an intimate and learned acquaintance with the ancient classics would at least require a lot of proof.

It is not likely to get it. Old Possum's biggest bluff has not waited till now to be called. Indeed, with all his wariness and 'ifs' and 'buts', he has given himself away more than once. There must surely be some relation between the scholarship of a poet and the poetry of scholarship. Eliot, writing of sermons on the Incarnation by Bishop Lancelot Andrewes,[1] preached before King James I, says that accordingly 'his erudition had full play; and his erudition is essential to his originality'. He continues—'Reading Andrewes on such a theme is like listening to a great Hellenist expounding a text of the *Posterior Analytics*: altering the punctuation, inserting or removing a comma or a semicolon to make an obscure passage suddenly luminous, dwelling on a single word, comparing its use in its nearer and its most remote contexts, purifying a disturbed or cryptic lecture-note into lucid profundity.' This is surely the observation of one who has missed nothing in the mind-straining, imagination-taxing, intricacies. It is one of the best give-aways; perhaps even a better example is a short note, openly, and, so far as I can see though I dare not compete, successfully, saying what the Greek word *logos* does *not* mean.[2]

Such classical knowledge is no outsider's knowledge. Outsider's knowledge can be very useful, not least to poets. Eliot is well aware that we can get something, and something legitimate, from poetry in a strange language when we cannot translate a single word of it.[3] Poets can so get a great deal, very usefully; even when they know the exact translation they normally need to set it off-centre for their purposes. Often enough Eliot depends on what might superficially

[1] *Selected Essays*, 1927, p. 337.

[2] *Ibid.*, p. 447, note 1; cf. the subtle choice of 'Gerontion', a name derived from a word in Aristophanes sharply different from 'Gerontius' in meaning.

[3] *Dante*, 1929, pp. 15–16; cf. Jeremy Jackson, p. 117 *supra*.

appear to be outsider's knowledge. A more general acquaintance[1] might have given him the majestic allusion to Agamemnon in 'Sweeney among the Nightingales', or an Aeschylean plot for *The Family Reunion*, or the self-contradictory Heracles of Euripides's *Alcestis*, whom no one even noticed to be behind Reilly in *The Cocktail Party*,[2] or even, conceivably, his comparison of Seneca's plays and Greek plays in their Stoicism or lack of it.[3] But no translation communicated the 'beauty of phrase' in Greek tragedies,[4] or 'verbal' beauty in Seneca,[5] or the effect on Seneca of the peculiar sensibility belonging to the Latin language,[6] or the close comparison of him in structure with Euripides and in prosody with the other Latin writers,[7] or the correction of an old error in rendering Seneca's *Hippolytus*, lines 1188–89.[8] The delightful observations of Seneca's 'crossing of one rhythm pattern with another' are not presented as newly made and original.[9] But the phenomena are of a kind to attract a scholar.

Eliot has himself[10] often enough emphasized the high value of the Greek and Latin classics for professional scholars, theologians and philosophers, historians and modern linguists, and for men of letters, and given some illuminating explanations. He would like everyone to learn Latin. He considers the classics necessary for the survival and development of a Christian civilization, and thinks that they should be permanently associated where they belong, with something permanent, the historical Christian faith. The classics must, of course, have a place in Eliot's important theory of poetic tradition,[11] which requires each poet to set himself in relation to all the dead poets, from Homer onwards, altering by his life and work the whole length and depth and meaning of total poetry. But I do not know of any

[1] Cf. *The Classics and the Man of Letters*, 1942, p. 10, for the utility of translations to poets.

[2] *Poetry and Drama*, 1951, pp. 31–2.

[3] *Selected Essays*, 1927, pp. 132–3.

[4] *Ibid.*, p. 67.

[5] *Ibid.*, p. 473.

[6] *Ibid.*, p. 67.

[7] *Ibid.*, p. 73.

[8] *Ibid.*, note 2.

[9] *Ibid.*, pp. 88–9.

[10] *Essays Ancient and Modern*, 1936, pp. 169–74; *The Classics and the Man of Letters*, *passim*, especially pp. 25–7.

[11] *Selected Essays*, 1927, pp. 13–22.

passage in which he has discussed the Greek and Latin classics at length as a special part or phase in this living and massive totality. There is, however, the notable address, *What is a Classic?*[1] Here Eliot observes several meanings of the word 'classic', and finds certain qualities which are necessary to any work deserving to be called 'a classic' in the narrowest, but still in a generally intelligible, sense. If Virgil turns out to be such a classic, or indeed the only such 'classic', that is partly because he lived and wrote in an age of 'classical' antiquity, and indeed the best age of classical antiquity for such an attainment. Maturity, manners and a certain bi-lingualism are especially wanted, and these requirements are met; but it had to be exactly then, and there, and by Virgil, 'the Father of the West'.

Eliot's defence of the classics is probably not yet fully published, and would no doubt be characteristically enlightening if it were continued, preferably in some contact with the thought of Fernand Robert's *L'Humanisme*.[2] But Eliot clearly enough says that the classics are useful to writers in general and readers in general. He even remarks that Shakespeare succeeded in spite of having little learning, and Milton succeeded in spite of having so much. But he does not say specifically that the classics are useful to poets as poets; or at least I remember no general argument to show why the later European poets have needed to use so much classical material. Eliot's own derivations are often very well fused and latent. But sometimes he declares his derivations. He openly based his dramatic work on Greek dramatists, Aristophanes, Aeschylus and Euripides, though he delayed announcing his use of Euripides in *The Cocktail Party* and, I believe, has not yet himself mentioned the obvious and well-known fact that *The Confidential Clerk* is a successor to the *Ion* of Euripides, and is much enriched by its choice of ancestry. Then there are the headings and notes, including a quotation from Lucian for 'Mr Apollinax', the fragments of Heraclitus which head *Burnt Norton*, the notable epigraph about the Sibyl to *The Waste*

[1] *What is a Classic?*, 1945.

[2] Fernand Robert, *L'Humanisme*, Essai de définition, Paris, Les Belles Lettres, 1946.

Land, and the long and intricate quotation from Ovid in the notes, concerning Tiresias, 'the most important personage in the poem'. These are not all;[1] but each is an example of a different kind of poetry inspired by a different kind of ancient quotation. Ovid is rather a poet's poet. His mythology continues to be needed by poets even though others may find it tedious. To digress, Eliot says that Dante used Virgil greatly but Ovid more.[2] It is attractive to wonder whether this is his own impression or the standard estimation taken as established. To form a new, and fair, estimate of this proportion in an otherwise preoccupied life must argue a very close knowledge of the texts of all three poets.

To try in a paragraph or two to disentangle truly 'classical' images and their operations would not be much use; it is, anyhow, the affair of others, one of whom will be mentioned later. But there are small observations to be made, and made fairly. Eliot creates or adopts images and symbols, of whatever origin—the 'leopard', the 'rocks', the 'still point of the turning world' and the rest. And he keeps them as an alphabet, as a signal-system, and uses them often, with or without verbal change. In *Ash-Wednesday* and poems following *Ash-Wednesday* there are several of these eloquently repeated images or symbols, and with them many rich systems of rhyme, pseudo-rhyme and assonance.[3] After these poems it is legitimate to note in the new, quieter, verse-movement of the *Four Quartets* a newly compressed verse-texture, with active metrical counterpoint. It is not fanciful to see in all this the help which Greek and Latin, and especially poetry in Latin, can give, and have greatly given, to a distant inheritor who has himself clearly spoken of such mechanisms in ancient verse.[4]

Not only did Eliot originally base his whole dramatic creation on ancient Greek drama, but his development as a dramatic poet, which he has himself modestly related,[5] has not been unlike the general

[1] Cf. Creedy (see note 1 on p. 119), pp. 46–8.

[2] *Dante*, p. 41.

[3] Cf. J. Landels, 'Poetae Anglici . . .', *Orpheus*, I, 1954, p. 41, for eloquent derivations, and also a line like a Latin hexameter in Eliot.

[4] *The Music of Poetry*, 1942, pp. 9–12.

[5] *Poetry and Drama, passim.*

history of drama at Athens. In both sequences the choral part becomes weaker and disappears. In both a verse-form near to, or indeed nearest to, the rhythm of prose-conversation is chosen, and at the end of the evolution there is less of the poetic in the content of the verse than there was at the beginning; Eliot thinks that there may be no poetry at all in his latest dramatic verse. The beginning is with Aristophanes and with Aeschylus, and Sweeney's furies are already Aeschylean—'You don't see them but I see them'; the same words occur again in *The Family Reunion.* In *The Cocktail Party* the most important motive belongs to what may well be an original shape of all Greek tragedy, but to us it is principally Sophoclean. This element is the aetiology of a hero-cult. Greek tragedy often re-enacts the events which led to the death of some ancient hero, who from then onwards enjoys a certain reverence and worship as a mighty spirit or saint. Oedipus had his faults. So did Celia. But both passed through anguish not only to peace but to sainthood. As Neville Braybrooke has said, what we are shown in *The Cocktail Party* is how a saint is made. A saint is also made in *Murder in the Cathedral.* And there, too, and in *The Rock* also, we are shown past events which have been the cause of important and lasting facts. Some of the facts are as broad and general as they are important. We learn, and are persuaded, that the Christian Faith survives opposition, and that the relations between Church and State are subject to intricate calculations both momentary and eternal, and yet dominated by a single Divine sanction. Not only do we see Saint Thomas attaining sainthood, but we also watch the foundations of our own order being laid, like the first audiences of Aeschylus. In this we can call the play Aeschylean. The dramatic characters of Aeschylus are individuals and, of course, well expressed. But we are left by Aeschylus not so much understanding and reverencing a single saint as reverencing and understanding the great forces in the human world, and the laws of God, which account for our good traditional institutions. This Aeschylean result belongs to Eliot's earlier plays; but it can be associated with the creation of a saint which is to us rather pre-Aeschylean, and also Sophoclean. So in *The Cocktail Party* the grand Sophoclean theme is interlaced with, or derived out of, the partly Euripidean Heracles-Reilly. There the characters themselves are already more Sophoclean. They are more sharply individualized psychopaths than their predecessors. There is more, too, in it than that. We are reminded, lightly perhaps, of a certain brilliant speciality in the characterization of Sophocles noticeable at least in the *Antigone*: his careful segregations not only of the heroic from the not-heroic, but also certain different sorts of the not-heroic from each other with almost equal care, and to some extent, too, the sorts of stronger personality of which the truly heroic is one. I think anyone who is willing first to compare the characters of *The Cocktail Party* and the characters of the *Antigone* with each other, and then to compare the two plays, will see what I mean.

Antigone herself in Sophocles is heroic, as Oedipus is heroic, in the sense propounded by Anouilh. But she is the plainest, clearest, simplest, least turgidly emotional, and least voluptuous of heroines. Sophocles exalts the poetry of her heroism by trying to make it cold prose. Euripides liked such a plain-fact style of thought and speech and used it more widely; and Eliot has done so, too. He has carried it very far, quite consciously, especially in *The Cocktail Party*, but also in lyrics, culminating in the remarkable Christmas poem about *The Cultivation of Christmas Trees*, 1954. This evolution towards a plain prose diction and phraseology in Eliot is comparable with the evolution in Greek tragedy; and though many other poets, some independent of Euripides, have also developed their style towards a light and even prosaic language in their later stages, in Eliot the light style, if these words will do for it, comes with other things which are still more Euripidean. *The Confidential Clerk* is about people who are not of high tragedy but more ordinary, and taken immediately from life. It is not necessary always to deal in what is, or one day will be, a momentous antiquity, which has left to the world or the city a divinely created order or a divinely created saint. It is not even necessary to end by implying on any important scale 'All shall be well'. 'All manner of things shall be well' might suggest a more appropriately limited meaning; or indeed nothing much need be well at all. What happens in *The Confidential Clerk* is a reflection from the *Ion* of Euripides; and both plays have an intriguing 'intrigue', and on the surface at least a not wholely unsympathetic satire. One more Euripidean tendency in Eliot may be mentioned. It is true that Euripides is often inclined to make speeches and dialogues lighter in style. But, of course, that is not all. For one thing, some of his speeches are elaborate oratory and may be quite technically rhetorical. Eliot's styles, especially his later styles, are not rhetorical, but in earlier dramas he is like Euripides in his free use of long speeches for persuasive argument on both sides of the question, when the question is of general interest and not essentially poetic or dramatic. *Murder in the Cathedral* contains probably all the best examples, including a sermon and speeches to the audience by the knights.

The Aeschylean tragedy of Orestes culminates in the establishment of the Court of the Areopagus, the great institution by which Athens brought the prerogatives of avenging ghosts, the ancestral Furies, within a human and general direction under law. Miss Maud Bodkin,[1] whose comparison of Eliot with Aeschylus should stand permanently, asks whether we have anything, or shall have anything, to correspond. When she wrote, in 1941, the future was still dark, but she considered the prospect of some effective world court in our own time to neutralize our present most dangerous Furies, the Furies of international war. From the text of *The Family Reunion* she cleverly argued that Eliot has not confined his dramatic experimentation strictly within the family, and that a world-wide solution for the wider problem is there sought. Since then there have been signs that the solution may in fact be found, and these Furies, too, may be brought within a human and divinely sanctioned law.

Father E. J. Stormon, SJ, has said that Aeschylus seems to him the strongest classical influence on Eliot. He said this in an article[2] in which he traced some of Eliot's many derivations from Virgil. There he mentions the Virgilian epigraph striking the keynote of the poem 'La Figlia che Piange', the description of the ragged rock in *The Dry Salvages*, the 'horned gate' in *Sweeney Agonistes*, the 'ivory gates' towards the end of *Ash-Wednesday* and much in *The Hollow*

[1] Maud Bodkin, *The Quest for Salvation in an Ancient and a Modern Play*, 1941, pp. 41–3.

[2] E. J. Stormon, SJ, 'Virgil and the Modern Poet', *Meanjin*, Melbourne, VI, Autumn 1947, pp. 6–15.

Men, including the conception of a soul purified under the 'deliberate disguise' of 'a scarecrow . . . behaving as the wind behaves'. But he maintains that still more important than the detailed reminiscences is the interest in time and its problems which is strong in both poets. The simultaneous perception of a time-dimension through which the past recedes and of a supra-temporal order in which the past never recedes finally involves an important aesthetic programme which has received its most satisfying formulation in Eliot's essay, 'Tradition and Individual Talent'. 'A sense of history does in fact play an important part in the poetry of men like Eliot and Yeats . . .' 'But for the perfect use of the time-dimension (not to speak of the past in its timeless aspect) we must go to Virgil. In the *Aeneid* it is everywhere . . .', especially 'in single forward- or backward-looking words or phrases and in a certain consciousness of "things gone by" conveyed by tone and texture as much as by explicit statement. The sense of time as a factor partly constitutive of the reality apprehended by the poet is something to which the modern should be particularly responsive. He will not find it in the Greeks (who have so much else to offer), and no other Latin has it in the same degree as Virgil.'

Yet when in the *Four Quartets* Eliot set most seriously to work, as D. W. Harding[1] put it, on the 're-creation of concepts' to define the intersection of the temporal and the timeless, he began by quoting Heraclitus. And indeed the re-creation of concepts is rather a Greek than a Latin adventure.[2] Eliot is ready for many influences and knows which is the right influence for his purpose. His most famous poem, *The Waste Land*, is headed by the Sibyl, and the heart of it is Ovid's Tiresias. When he explores the destiny of the soul beyond death he starts with Plato and other well-chosen sources, eastern and western, for there is security in orthodox form. Like Kipling, of whom he uses the words, Eliot himself is not unaware of what lies behind and beyond the veil:

> And what the dead had no speech for, when living,
> They can tell you, being dead: the communication
> Of the dead is tongued with fire beyond the language of the living.

[1] *Scrutiny*, V, September 1936.
[2] Cf. Creedy, pp. 48–58, for the wide use made of Greek philosophy.

But he accepts the classical contour. His poems are things made, things meant to exist by themselves. That is, they are not mere jotted messages, handing on, for information, anything in immediate experience happening to be noticed, however sure, however profound. The classical poets must find and use, and use in harmony together and in transmissive growth, their form.

I hope that I shall not be ignorantly accused of ending not with a cheer but a titter if I choose for my end-piece quotation something which shows the intimacy in which Eliot possesses classical things, and words, and names. 'The Naming of Cats', he says, 'is a difficult matter.' Names such as Peter, Augustus, Alonzo or James can be given. But—

> There are fancier names if you think they sound sweeter,
> Some for the gentlemen, some for the dames:
> Such as Plato, Admetus, Electra, Demeter—
> But all of them sensible everyday names.

And indeed they are—to T. S. Eliot.

T. S. Eliot as a Translator

VINCENT CRONIN

TRANSLATION is a word with a negative charge, and to translators we tend to ascribe a status somewhere between those of cipher clerk and midwife. Dangerous condescension, which flies in face of the facts. What was the Renaissance in literature but the translation of certain Greek and Latin books? To take only two examples, if the *Thousand and One Nights* had remained in Arabic, much of the best of Chaucer would never have been written; and but for the existence of North's Plutarch, translations of Italian *novelle* and other Romance works, Shakespeare might be remembered as a sonneteer.

The word itself is partly to blame, for it conceals the translator's most important business, namely his selection of a foreign text. The primary sense of 'translate' is to remove to another place. Only secondarily does it mean to turn from one language into another. I think that these two definitions can be usefully amalgamated into a third, which may enhance the status of the word. According to this wider definition a translator is one who transfers part of the civilization of one country to the civilization of another, and it is in this sense that I propose first of all to use the term of T. S. Eliot. Examples of the word in this sense are Kipling in his *Jungle Books* and FitzGerald, who made not a literal rendering of Omar Khayyam's *Rubaiyat* but an adaptation which includes Persian traditions absent from the original stanzas.

Eliot began to translate as soon as he began to write poetry at Harvard. The important thing about Harvard for a young artist is not so much its European traditions as its open-mindedness towards contemporary European currents. Just as immigrants surge, in quotas, through the port of Boston, so their ideas invade Harvard and, indeed, all New England. It was here that Melville had absorbed and turned to good account the German metaphysicians; Longfellow, Sir Walter Scott and Emerson the German Transcendentalists with their tincture of Brahmanism. To say that Eliot started writing at Harvard virtually implies that he adopted a recent European mode.

His choice fell on France. The meeting between Eliot and French poetry of the late Nineteenth Century was arranged by a go-between: Arthur Symons's book *The Symbolist Movement in Literature*. This type of book is, in the wide sense, translation and, it may be noticed in passing, of greater value than is usually admitted; without it imaginative writers, either through lack of time, fluency in foreign languages or the appropriate books might otherwise miss the originals. What Symons did was to introduce Eliot to Laforgue. As Eliot has said:[1] 'The form in which I began to write, in 1908 or 1909, was directly drawn from the study of Laforgue together with the later Elizabethan drama.'

Two things about Jules Laforgue are relevant here. Though brought up in the French provinces, he was born in Montevideo; coming from the New World, he saw the Old with the wonder and objectivity of one who did not quite belong. Secondly, his dates: born 1860, died 1887. When Eliot discovered him, Laforgue had been dead over twenty years. In France, at least, he would no longer have been considered *avant-garde*.

Laforgue's characteristics are irony as an escape from moral suffering; juxtaposition of the trivialities of present-day life with extremely serious topics to heighten the effect of the latter; in form, the interior monologue, repetition of key-words and rhyme as ironic emphasis.

Laforgue's chief innovation perhaps only an American could develop. At any rate, Eliot did develop it until it became one of his hallmarks. In his poems before 1930 Eliot can be said to be applying to poetics the principles of the American constitution. In effect he proclaims: 'There are no longer a chosen few themes. All subjects are equal, all have a right to be poetry. The poet must learn to sing of "stony rubbish", to beat even the dustbin lid as a cymbal.'

[1] Introduction to Ezra Pound's *Selected Poems*, 1928.

At first Laforgue's influence showed itself in pastiche, for example 'Humouresque (after J. Laforgue)' in the *Harvard Advocate* during 1910. The decisive turning-point came when Eliot spent the year 1910–11 in Paris. Here he lived over Laforgue's discovery of France and gained that intimacy with the French language without which Laforgue could never deeply penetrate his work.

Eliot has compared the influence of one poet over another to demonic possession. These are strong words from one who does not use words lightly. I believe that in using this simile Eliot had Laforgue in mind, and that it must be taken at face value.

A whole monograph would be needed in order to determine, in Eliot's first two books, how much is word-for-word translation and how much totally original. What Eliot himself implies is that in some of this poetry, both as regards style and subject-matter, there is more of Laforgue than of himself, and it is therefore proper to speak of translation in the wide sense of the term. It is to be noted that in at least two of the poems, *Preludes* and 'Rhapsody on a Windy Night', the language is nearer to translated French than to idiomatic English.

In *The Waste Land* Laforgue is much less evident. He died at the age of twenty-seven and remains a young man's poet, capable of influencing only the young. *The Waste Land*, by contrast, both in mood and its framework of anthropology and cosmology, is nothing if not adult. But of this work, too, translation forms an integral part. Word-for-word renderings, paraphrases of and allusions to foreign texts and actual foreign quotations are used to an extent unequalled since the Renaissance. Indeed, the success of the poem can be largely traced to a close and fruitful tension between Eliot the creative poet and Eliot the translator.

Direct translations become fewer in Eliot's later work but never altogether disappear, a well-known example being Mallarmé's aphorism in *Little Gidding*: 'To purify the language of the tribe.' His thought continues to be permeated by modern French writers, including Baudelaire and Rémy de Gourmont, from whom many of Eliot's critical principles stem. Not that his attention is confined to France. James, Pound and Eliot—like the eclectic Romans of the Early Empire they treat all Europe as their province.

So powerful was the early ascendancy of Laforgue that it almost made of Eliot a French poet. I am thinking of the four French poems he included in *Poems 1920*. Though it is feasible to think in a familiar foreign tongue, I doubt whether anyone who has not learned the language as a small child can conceive poetically in any language but his own. Though the originals of these four poems were doubtless never written down in English, it seems fairly certain that they were conceived in that language, and must therefore be considered translations of an unusual kind.

A reason can be found why each of the four should have been written in French rather than in English. In 'Le Directeur', which reads like a sophisticated nursery rhyme, Eliot plays on sonorities strictly speaking French. 'Mélange Adultère de Tout' presents the cosmopolitan *déraciné* with irony bordering on surrealism; it breathes the very spirit of the Left Bank, for which French is clearly the appropriate medium. 'Lune de Miel' owes its inspiration to'Veder Napoli poi morir' by an exact contemporary of Laforgue, the Breton, Tristan Corbière. Dry and salty, with a certain grossness permissible in French but not, perhaps, in English, the poem contains one of the most striking images in all Eliot:

> Et Sainte Apollinaire, raide et ascétique,
> Vieille usine désaffectée de Dieu.

In the last poem of this series, 'Dans le Restaurant', an old waiter tells of his first erotic awakening at the age of seven. Sordid and scabrous, it is chiefly notable for its last seven lines—the image of Phlebas the drowned Phoenician—which in English (with few changes) form Part IV of *The Waste Land*. If the poems were written in the order in which they were published, here is a curious instance of a poet translating one of his own translations back into English. In conclusion, all four French poems are remarkable for their idiomatic wit and intimate knowledge of French—not the Academicians' language but 'as she is spoke'.

I now turn to Eliot's work in the *Criterion*. The strength of this periodical was that it ranged so widely as to be virtually international. It published *comptes rendus* of foreign reviews (including even

Danish). Its editorials made known contemporary foreign intellectual movements. In 1924 it sponsored a translation in book form of *A Brief Introduction to the Method of Paul Valéry* with a preface by Eliot. It published foreign writing in translation, such as Thomas Mann's 'An Appeal to Reason'. Eliot himself contributed six translations from French into English.

Of these the first two were contributions by Charles Mauron and Ramon Fernandez to a debate arising from an article in the *Criterion* early in 1927 by John Middleton Murry. Murry had advocated a new classicism based on a synthesis of Intuition and Intelligence. Mauron retorted that intuition was nothing but a catchword, and Fernandez argued that 'either the qualitative intuition is not knowledge, but simply a *presentiment* of knowledge based on an impression *sui generis*; or else it tends to justify itself by transforming itself into rational knowledge'. With these two translations Eliot brought the precise clarity of French thought to bear on a vague concept and, by raising the debate from coterie level, helped to make its issues more tractable.

Eliot's next translation was 'Prologue to An Essay on Criticism' by Charles Maurras. Maurras contends that the occupations of creative art and criticism are exactly the same: the only real difference is in the subject-matter. This essay is a somewhat tedious and pontifical 'Hurrah for Criticism!', more concerned with the dignity and trappings of the critic than with analysing what manner of man he is. Perhaps Eliot translated it because the exhortations of a highly esteemed French writer to pursue the classical tradition and return to Malherbe lent weight to his own principles of criticism.

In the *Criterion* for December 1928 Eliot revealed himself in one of his most useful roles as translator. He introduced to the English public a virtually unknown foreign writer. 'Fustel de Coulanges', by Pierre Gaxotte, is an appreciation of one who, with Taine, ranks among the most important French historians of the Nineteenth Century. Here, as in all these six articles, Eliot has clearly decided to translate because he sympathizes profoundly with the subject-matter: Coulanges in his chief work, *L'Histoire des Institutions politiques de l'ancienne France*, shows religion and love of the past to be the twin forces at work in history. A point of curiosity in this translation is that the ice of Eliot's prose cracks for the duration of a single phrase: 'Fustel blew the gaff on republican sentimentality.'

Thirteen months later the *Criterion* published Eliot's translation of 'A Humanist Theory of Value', by Ramon Fernandez. Fernandez points to a fundamental contradiction in humanism, 'which subordinates desires to values and at the same time makes values depend upon human custom'. This, the most important of Eliot's prose translations, was followed by Charles Mauron's 'On Reading Einstein', an unconvincing attempt to show that Einstein's discovery deepens the gulf between mystical and scientific knowledge. Again, perhaps Eliot recognized its shortcomings and printed it in support of a favourite theory: that an educated man should be as familiar with the latest findings of natural science as with the most recent style of Picasso. Of these prose translations in the *Criterion*, it can be said that they are precise and accurate. If the prose is cold, the style dry, these are criticisms of the originals not of the translation. None of the articles is a work of art, none likely to endure, but at the time their appearance was useful in keeping English readers abreast of French thought.

I now turn to Eliot's most important translation. By the time *The Hollow Men* appeared in 1925, Eliot had evidently worked out the seam laid bare by Laforgue; he stood in need of new imagery. For the second time he found it in France. Eliot had always been closely linked with the *Nouvelle Revue Française* and he doubtless read a short book published by that house as soon as it appeared in 1925. The book was *Anabase*, by Saint-John Perse.

Saint-John Perse is the pseudonym of Marie-René-Auguste-Alexis Léger. Like Laforgue, he was born outside France, in 1887, at Saint-Léger-les-Feuilles, a small island near Guadeloupe. When Alexis Léger was twelve, his family moved to Pau: a formative change which perhaps accounts for the poet's preoccupation with travel and his nostalgia for distant places. Gide thought so highly of Léger's early verse that he paid the publication expenses of *Eloges* (1911). In that year Alain-Fournier met him (and perhaps reported his impressions to Eliot, a close friend). Léger he describes as short and fattish, very tense and inclined to be solemn: an admirer of Laforgue's spare, cursive diction. In unconscious prophecy of *Anabase*, Alain-Fournier adds that Léger would be 'even more extraordinary, more mysterious, if he were more simple'.

In 1914 Léger entered the diplomatic corps. During his service at the Legation in Peking, he explored the Gobi Desert on horseback. In 1921 he chose his well-known pseudonym, out of affection for the elliptical, concentrated style of the Roman poet Persius. In 1924 he published in the periodical *Commerce* a translation of Eliot's *The Hollow Men.* After the appearance of *Anabase* for seventeen years Léger published nothing, and none of his recent work equals that poem in importance. In 1933 Léger was appointed Secretary-General of the French Foreign Office. Unlike Claudel, he never became an ambassador, though he was known as a sort of modern *éminence grise.* A passion for anonymity is typical also of his poetry: *Anabase* reveals practically nothing about its author; even the 'people' it purports to describe are never identified—in fact they remain unidentifiable.

I hope I am neither forcing a paradox nor riding a hobby-horse in claiming that *Anabase*, one of the most original poems in European literature, owes its originality chiefly to translations; among them, the Egyptian Book of the Dead, Vedic hymns and inscriptions from Asiatic steles. Under the influence of these translations (available only comparatively recently), *Anabase* reverts to a period when law, ritual and chant were mingled, when men were types, not yet individualized. As for the style—almost religiously solemn—it, too, belongs to the period, when words were written down for such purposes as to frame laws or enumerate objects in the treasury, more often than not engraved; hence the concision—*on ne bavarde pas sur la pierre.* Perse deliberately removes logical connections, so that words, isolated, ring alone instead of in the carillon of a descriptive sentence. Like every artist, he still selects, but not according to classical or indeed any known rules. He presents raw materials—like an archaeologist's finds—from which the reader must construct a whole civilization.

It is to Eliot's credit that he immediately recognized the significance of so original a poem and repaid his debt to French literature by translating it: a difficult task, though not for the usual reasons. There were no rhymes (though much assonance), no strict metre, no specifically French allusions. The difficulty lay in the poem's concision. The over-tones of the French words echoed across the logical gaps: could this be achieved in English without making the poem impossibly obscure? Few will doubt that Eliot has succeeded: though the English text has to be read more often than the French to yield its meaning. The other prime merit of Eliot's version is that it captures the rhythm of the original: extremely long lines hovering, even in French, very close to prose.

In at least two places Eliot improves on the French: the important last words of Part IV: '*marchand de flacons*' become 'dealer in scent-bottles'. Elsewhere '*l'écorce du monde*' is made unforgettable as 'the wrinkled rind of the world'. On the other hand, I have three quarrels with Eliot's version. In Part I he writes 'Our burnished arms are fair in the morning and behind us the sea is fair'. 'Behind us' has no justification in the French text, and later (in Part IV), when the city is founded, reference is made to the election of harbour-masters. If their journey was towards the sea, I don't understand how this Central Asian people could have had the sea *behind* them when they started. Again, '*l'oiseau chante : ô vieillesse !*' becomes 'the bird sings O Senectus !'—clearly an attempt to avoid the impossible 'O old age !' But this pronounced Latinism jars badly in a deliberately 'barbarian' poem. Another word which I think jars is a single rendering of 'cavaliers' by the same word in English (elsewhere Eliot translates it as 'horsemen').

Part I of the translated poem appeared in the *Criterion* for February 1928. Between this version and the text of the first edition are a dozen changes, nearly all in the direction of greater exactitude. Perhaps they were the result of Perse's own recommendations. '*Mathématiques*', for instance, is changed from 'geometry' to 'calculations', and '*du songe, notre aînesse*' from 'the primogeniture of dream' to 'our entail of dream'. The hazy, romantic translation of the last words: 'drawing to our ways the keels unforgotten unforgettable' (the French has 'immortelles carènes') is improved to 'drawing to our dockyards eternal keels'.

So much for Eliot's text. The chief influence of *Anabase* in the last thirty years has been upon the translator's own poetry. Eliot himself has admitted[1] that Perse's poem directly suggested the lines in 'Journey of the Magi' (1927):

> There were times we regretted
> The summer palaces on slopes, the terraces;
> And the silken girls bringing sherbet.

A more important result was a shift towards a lapidary style in which the poet's own point of view is suggested rather than stated, and from urban, specifically twentieth-century imagery to the timeless symbols, first of the desert and, in *Four Quartets*, of the four elements. To be aware of the change one has only to turn from *The Waste Land* to such lines as the following from *Ash-Wednesday* (1930):

> Under a tree in the cool of the day, with the blessing of sand,
> Forgetting themselves and each other, united
> In the quiet of the desert.

What, in conclusion, can be inferred of Eliot the translator? With the highest technical proficiency he has played four very different roles, of which the second and third were directed towards furthering a common European tradition. The first and fourth are more important and were central to his development as a poet; indeed, at the beginning of his career translator and poet were so intimately linked as to be scarcely distinguishable. His decision to render *Anabase* was a crucial decision in English literature. This work, like the translations of other major creative artists—D. H. Lawrence's versions of Verga and Proust's of Ruskin—has proved primarily fruitful to his own art, though there is no reason to think that its influence or that of the earliest poems will be limited for very long. Just as great new churches were built on the translated bodies of foreign saints, so, too, we may expect new English verse—as distinct from pastiche—to arise on Eliot's translations of Laforgue and Saint-John Perse.

[1] *T. S. Eliot et la France*, by Edward Green, 1951.

T. S. Eliot as a Political Writer

J. M. CAMERON

MR ELIOT has never been deficient in candour and the courage to criticize himself. Ten years ago he remarked somewhat acidly on 'the tendency . . . for those who have acquired some reputation, to write books outside the subject on which they have made their reputation';[1] and did not hesitate to instance his own work. Here he is unjust to himself. Even if he had never written a word about politics, it would still be evident that the author of *Coriolan* and *Murder in the Cathedral* had reflected much upon the life of our society and upon the relations of Church and State. Apart from this, Mr Edwin Muir's comment on the politics of Shakespeare applies very well to Mr Eliot. Mr Muir writes:

> It has been maintained that Shakespeare had no politics. Now this may be true in a sense, if it means that he cannot be put down as a Conservative, or a Liberal, or a Socialist, or whatever the counterparts of these modern classifications were in his time . . . But a man may have political sense, and political sense of a high kind, without falling into any of these categories; for his mind, while working politically, may not think in terms of any of them. To say that Shakespeare had no politics—if one takes the statement seriously—can only mean that he had no conception of what is good in society; and to assert that would bring an immediate denial from everybody. It has been said that he was above the conflict; it would be more true to say that he was above the classification.[2]

The nerve of all Mr Eliot's work has been his feeling and his concern for the human good. From *Prufrock*, through *The Waste Land*, to the *Four Quartets*, this feeling and this concern give strength and passion to the most remarkable English verse of our time. To recognize this is not to fall into the error, often noticed by Mr Eliot,

[1] *Notes Towards the Definition of Culture*, 1948, p. 86.
[2] Edwin Muir, *Essays on Literature and Society*, 1949, p. 32.

of appraising poetry by moral or religious criteria, but simply to note that high achievement in poetry comes to an integrated man who, as it were, has digested and absorbed the life of his time.[1]

We encounter Shakespeare as a political mind only in *King Lear*, say, or *Coriolanus* or the historical plays. But Mr Eliot has written a great many essays which contain political remarks and has written directly upon political themes in, for example, the Commentaries in the *Criterion* and in such works as *The Idea of a Christian Society* and *Notes Towards the Definition of Culture*. Here he is perhaps more in the tradition of French and American than of English letters; and one is inclined to think that, despite the generous tributes he so often pays to Tawney, Demant, Christopher Dawson and other English writers, the deeper influences have been such writers as Irving Babbitt, Paul Elmer More and Charles Maurras. No one wholly English in culture could have brought himself in the nineteen-twenties to confess to 'Royalism' as a political creed;[2] and though the Anglo-Catholicism with which Mr Eliot linked his Royalism is by definition English, as worn by him it has a less insular cut than is common. This slight eccentricity to English styles of thinking has sometimes been of, though not always, immense advantage to Mr Eliot in his political writings. In the heady days of the Popular Front he managed to keep his balance when many writers lost theirs,[3] and this without yielding to the complacency which marked the Conservatism of Mr Chamberlain and Lord Halifax.[4]

[1] 'While the practice of poetry need not in itself confer wisdom or accumulate knowledge, it ought at least to train the mind in one habit of universal value: that of analysing the meanings of words.' *The Idea of a Christian Society*, 1939, p. 8. This is true; but such a capacity could bring the poet to no more than pedantry if it stood by itself.

[2] In *For Lancelot Andrewes*, 1928, Preface.

[3] Cf. 'The delusion of the "Popular Front", which is so seductive to the intelligentsia of every country.' *Criterion*, Vol. XVI, No. lxiv, April 1937, p. 474.

[4] Cf. 'I believe that there must be many persons who, like myself, were deeply shaken by the events of September 1938, in a way from which one does not recover; persons to whom that month brought a profounder realization of the general plight. It was not a disturbance of the understanding: the events themselves were not surprising. Nor, as became increasingly evident, was our distress due merely to disagreement with the policy and behaviour of the moment. The feeling which was new and unexpected was a feeling of humiliation, which seemed to demand an act of personal contrition, of humility, repentance and amendment;

Mr Eliot has in his political writings two main themes: Culture, and Church and State. He has written from time to time on political philosophy, and has frequently deplored the absence from contemporary English politics of any political philosophy; but by political philosophy he means not so much the analytical study of political concepts—our greatest practitioner in this field is certainly Thomas Hobbes, and he does not find Hobbes a sympathetic thinker[1]—as political *Weltanschauung*;[2] and political philosophy in this sense is an ingredient of culture as Mr Eliot understands it rather than a critical study of the second-order questions (that is, meta-political questions) that arise out of reflection upon the terminology and concepts employed in political discourse. As a Christian thinker he is more interested in getting the right answers to political questions than in the appraisal of the logical relations between concepts. It is true, these two enterprises have historically—and rightly—been run together; but the latter is the truly philosophical enterprise. At any rate, Mr Eliot is concerned about what is wrong with our society: the decay of religious belief, the vulgarization of culture, the bankruptcy of Protestant theology—he has never seemed much impressed by the Dialectical Theology of continental neo-Calvinism—the decline in natural piety as this decline shows itself in the commercial exploitation of natural resources and contempt for the past, the growing flatness and imprecision of language. It is impossible to go through

what had happened was something in which one was deeply implicated and responsible. . . . Was our society, which had always been so assured of its superiority and rectitude, so confident of its unexamined premisses, assembled round anything more permanent than a congeries of banks, insurance companies and industries, and had it any beliefs more essential than a belief in compound interest and the maintenance of dividends?' *The Idea of a Christian Society*, p. 64.

[1] See the essay on Bramhall, in *Essays Ancient and Modern*, 1936. Hobbes is described as 'an extraordinary little upstart', and as 'undoubtedly an atheist'. The former point is a matter of opinion, but the latter is by no means undoubted. My own view is that Hobbes is certainly a believer, having affinities with both Socinianism and Calvinism, and deriving much from the Nominalism of the later Middle Ages. He was probably a 'mortalist', but almost certainly not an atheist.

[2] Cf. 'What I mean by a political philosophy is not merely even the conscious formulation of the ideal aims of a people, but the substratum of collective temperament, ways of behaviour and unconscious values which provides the material for the formulation.' *The Idea of a Christian Society*, p. 18.

the files of the *Criterion* without coming to know both the breadth and the particularity of Mr Eliot's interest in the signs of barbarism and cultural decay. Nothing is too small or too trivial for his attention: the protection of wild birds,[1] the preservation of the squares and enclosures of London,[2] the fate of the City churches.[3] Equally, he has something to say, though his pessimism grows darker throughout the 'thirties, on the great problems of which the smaller barbarisms are no more than symptoms.[4]

Mr Eliot is convinced—no doubt he owes in part this conviction to the work of Mr Christopher Dawson—that religion is the vital element in culture; and he is equally convinced that the matter to be attended to in the consideration of religion is the question of truth and not the question of utility or aesthetic quality.[5] There is, all the same, a problem to be solved, an ambiguity to be teased out, in what Mr Eliot has from time to time written about religion and culture; and it has a direct bearing on what is for him the central political problem, the relations of Church and State, as I shall try to show.

One aspect of his thought on these matters is well represented by the notorious avowal of his belief in Royalism, Classicism and Anglo-Catholicism in the Preface to the volume *For Lancelot Andrewes*, and by the essay 'Lancelot Andrewes' in the same volume. Of course, he was to remark later that this running together of political views, critical prejudices and religious belief was liable to mislead the reader, adding that 'I now see the danger of suggesting to outsiders [only?] that the Faith is a political principle or a literary fashion, and the sum of all a dramatic posture'.[6] But the notorious sentence in the Preface is not the only, nor the most important,

[1] *Monthly Criterion*, Vol. VI, No. iii, September 1927.

[2] *Ibid.*

[3] *New Criterion*, Vol. V, No. i, January 1927.

[4] E.g., he censures 'urbanization of mind' and the indifference of the major parties to the problem of rural depopulation, adding: 'One sees no hope either in the Labour Party or in the equally unimaginative dominant section of the Conservative Party. There seems no hope in contemporary politics at all.' *Criterion*, Vol. XVIII, No. lxx, October 1938.

[5] 'What is worst of all is to advocate Christianity, not because it is true, but because it might be beneficial.' *The Idea of a Christian Society*, p. 58.

[6] *After Strange Gods: A Primer of Modern Heresy*, 1934, p. 28.

passage which suggests a view of the function of Christianity in culture which has certain affinities with the views of Maurras.[1] In 'Lancelot Andrewes' he tells us that 'the Church of England is the creation of the reign of Elizabeth. The *via media* which is the spirit of Anglicanism was the spirit of Elizabeth in all things'. He speaks of the Church of England as 'a masterpiece of ecclesiastical statesmanship'. It is true, he adds the proviso that 'we must not confuse the history of a Church with its spiritual meaning'; nevertheless, 'a Church is to be judged by its intellectual fruits, by its influence on the sensibility of the most sensitive and on the intellect of the most intelligent, and it must be made real to the eye by monuments of artistic merit'. And: 'No religion can survive the judgment of history unless the best minds of its time have collaborated in its construction. . . .' No matter what provisos may be added, the terms employed are such as to imply what may be called the connoisseur's conception of religion. The criteria of judgment invoked are intellectual and aesthetic; the capacity of a Church to survive 'the judgment of history' (is this to be understood as human or as Divine judgment?) rests upon human achievement—the willingness of 'the best minds' to collaborate. Just as Maurras, the unbeliever, commended Catholicism on account of its organic connection with Roman and French history (and regretted the supreme claim made by the Catholic Church to the obedience of men, for the essence of this claim is that the Church is the New Israel, and thus to be a Christian is to be spiritually a Semite); so Mr Eliot appears to be suggesting that the primary claim of the Church of England upon our attention is derived from its cultural achievements. All this has an air of paradox; for the grounds upon which Mr Eliot here seems to be commending the Church of England are precisely those which have been stressed by unfriendly critics as witnessing to the merely human character of that institution. What is there in what Mr Eliot here says that differs radically from the massive indictment brought by Newman against his old communion? Newman countered the argu-

[1] In reply to a suggestion that the intention of Maurras had been 'to pervert his disciples and students away from Christianity', Mr Eliot wrote: 'I have been a reader of the work of Maurras for eighteen years; upon me he has had exactly the opposite effect.' *Monthly Criterion*, Vol. VII, No. iii, March 1928, p. 202.

ments of those who urged that the Church of England must in some sense be a part of the Catholic Church, pointing as evidence of this to its vitality, by alleging that they confused the energy of a great secular and national institution with the life of the spirit. Anglicanism (he writes) is 'the religion of gentlemen, of scholars, of men of substance, and men of no religion at all. If this be life [then] it be life to impart a tone to the court and houses of parliament, to ministers of state, to law and literature, to universities and schools, and to society'.[1] Of course, even in 'Lancelot Andrewes' Mr Eliot is aware that the 'spiritual meaning'—an unhappy phrase, for no institution is quite without spiritual meaning—of the Church of England is not to be exhausted by an account of Anglican history and culture from the reign of Elizabeth down to our own day; but to give to intellectual and aesthetic fruits such a degree of importance as he wishes to give them is theologically extremely odd—as though one were to commend Catholicism to the French of our own day by pointing to the excellence of Bossuet's prose.[2]

One conjectures that Mr Eliot very soon perceived that the meaning most naturally put upon his theological and political views as they were expressed in *For Lancelot Andrewes* was not one he wished to defend. He made handsome amends five years later in *After Strange Gods*.[3] Yet it is this work, magnificently contemptuous in its reflections upon a society 'worm-eaten with Liberalism',[4] which contains a passage perhaps closer in spirit to the writings of Maurras —and one which sounded extremely offensive in the acoustics of the

[1] John Henry Newman, *Lectures on Anglican Difficulties*, Second Edition, 1850, p. 40.

[2] It ought to be made clear that the present writer is a Roman Catholic; but he thinks he would be inclined to say very much the same thing, though he might put it somewhat differently, were he an Anglican.

[3] See especially pp. 27, 28.

[4] *Ibid.*, p. 13. He later observed acutely, in connection with the vogue of communism among the intellectuals of the 'thirties, that 'communism flourished because it grew so easily on the Liberal root'. *Criterion*, Vol. XVIII, No. lxx, October 1938, p. 272. This, of course, is communism as an intellectual fashion, the communism of the salon. Communism as a political movement—at least, as one with indigenous sources of strength—has *flourished* only in such countries as Russia and China. The communist voters of such countries as Italy and France are delusive phenomena; the revolution they seem to portend is a mirage.

year of publication (1934)—than anything else to be found in his writings.

> You are hardly likely to develop tradition except where the bulk of the population is relatively so well off where it is that it has no incentive or pressure to move about. The population should be homogeneous; where two or more cultures exist in the same place they are likely either to be fiercely self-conscious or both to become adulterate. What is still more important is unity of religious background; and reasons of race and religion combine to make any large number of free-thinking Jews undesirable. . . . And a spirit of excessive tolerance is to be deprecated.[1]

It can scarcely be doubted that in his reference to the 'free-thinking Jews' Mr Eliot is echoing the *Maurrassien* teaching on the role of the *métèque* in a society 'worm-eaten with Liberalism'.[2]

One would not wish to criticize Mr Eliot simply on the ground that he has taken over from Maurras a doctrine which, from the days of the *Affaire*, has been used to give an appearance of respectability to violence, injustice and blasphemy. Such a doctrine may exaggerate a true doctrine, be a heresy; and since people are often deaf, it may in some circumstances be necessary to shout. But two considerations strike me as being apposite. First, such a doctrine is so closely connected with the vicissitudes of the Third French Republic that it is hard to see—certainly, Mr Eliot does not enlighten us—its relevance to English or American conditions. The social evils of both countries are manifold; but it would be hard to show that these evils flowed from the role of the *métèques* in educational, artistic or political life. This view would run into particular difficulties as an analysis of American society; and it is American society that Mr Eliot has primarily in mind in the first of the lectures in *After Strange Gods*. '*Métèque*' is, after all, a relative term, and too generous a use of the term would transform the vast majority of the inhabitants of the United States into *métèques*, and would raise the interesting question whether the Puritans of New England are entitled to call the Anglicans of Virginia *métèques*, or the Anglicans the Puritans. If we are to have as fine a nose as Maurras for the

[1] *After Strange Gods*, pp. 19, 20.

[2] Another echo: Mr Eliot can say of Virginia that it has been less industrialized and *less invaded by foreign races*! *Ibid.*, p. 16. My italics.

foreign infection, we shall in looking at American society be compelled to treat such names as Roosevelt, Eisenhower and McCarthy as being pre-eminently signs of the presence of the *métèques* in political life. Secondly, such a remark about the Jews as Mr Eliot permits himself in these lectures (delivered at the University of Virginia in 1933 and published in 1934) has a peculiar resonance when we recall that the year 1933 was the year in which Hitler and his party made themselves the masters of Germany and called upon 'reasons of race', if not of religion, to justify the most cruel and bloody persecution known to history.[1]

Altogether, one is inclined to suggest that Mr Eliot's appearance as a softened and domesticated Maurras, the Maurras of Anglo-Saxon liberal society, sprang from a failure—a failure fully shared by those liberal and communist intellectuals who were the first to censure Mr Eliot—to perceive that the advent of totalitarianism had raised moral and political questions of an entirely new kind. Modern industrial societies are such that counter-revolution in the name of tradition, hierarchy, the defence of religion, the preservation of the national community and so on produces exactly the same consequences as revolution in the name of progress, equality, emancipation from religion, internationalism and so on. Hitler and Stalin are faces on opposite sides of the same coin. What is surprising is that Mr Eliot fails to see that his real affinities are not with Maurras (so radical in his positivism) but with those who are the prophets and apologists of the liberal societies of England and the United States: with Jefferson and Burke, with Acton and Maitland.[2]

[1] Hindsight is, of course, easy. But the general intentions of the Nazis were known before 1933; the furnaces of Auschwitz were already on the drawing-board.

[2] Mr Eliot tends to underestimate the toughness of the English political tradition. After arguing that in Italy a pagan theory of the State is modified by the tradition of society in 'a country which is still mainly agricultural and Catholic', he goes on to say: 'The more highly industrialized the country, the more easily a materialistic philosophy will flourish in it, and the more deadly that philosophy will be. Britain has been highly industrialized longer than any other country. And the tendency of unlimited industrialism is to create bodies of men and women—of all classes—detached from tradition, alienated from religion and susceptible to mass suggestion: in other words, a mob.' *The Idea of a Christian Society*, p. 21. Even if one is inclined to agree with Mr Eliot's generalization, at

All this is no more than an episode in the development of Mr Eliot's political thought. In *The Idea of a Christian Society* the *Maurrassien* note is scarcely struck; and in the *Definition of Culture* —the best and wisest of the books in this vein—it is quite vanished. But the episode is, all the same, significant; for the episode was only possible on account of an ambiguity in Mr Eliot's conception of the Church. To care so desperately about culture, and about a particular historic culture, that the Church ceases to be even in principle detachable from the culture, and may even, as with Maurras, be valued solely by reason of its links with and its social and political role within the culture, this is to neglect what may be called the transcendence of the Church and to overemphasize the immanence of the Church; as did the late Hilaire Belloc in *Europe and the Faith.* How far Mr Eliot has clarified his view of the Church (even in Anglican terms), and thus placed himself in a position to deal satisfactorily with the problem of Church and State, we must now enquire.

The central contention of *The Idea of a Christian Society* is, I take it, that 'a liberalized or negative condition of society must either proceed into a gradual decline of which we can see no end, or . . . reform itself into a positive shape which is likely to be effectively secular'; and the only alternative to decline or secular reform is 'a positive Christian society'.[1] The present writer would not wish to quarrel with this. Now, granted the possibility and the desirability of a positive Christian society, the enquirer, whether Christian or not, is likely to ask for a sketch, if not for a blueprint; and one feature of the sketch will have to be a few lines which suggest the place of the

a level high enough and over a time long enough, its application to the English people is doubtful. It must be harder to raise a mob in England than in any other country of western Europe, and the thing which strikes observers from Europe is the English capacity for co-operation and self-discipline. Mr Eliot, for all his interest in the Seventeenth Century, has never read the paradoxical lesson of that period: that the victory of the Puritans over the Monarchy was the condition for the survival in England, alone of the European countries, of a medieval and Catholic tradition in the State and in Law. This is the grain of truth in the Whig interpretation of history. It seems unlikely that the victory of the Anglican Counter-Reformation under Andrewes and Laud would have produced results of which Mr Eliot would have approved.

[1] *The Idea of a Christian Society*, p. 25.

Church, both as the community of Christians and as an hierarchical institution, in the Christian State. Mr Eliot rejects the idea that such a relation is best founded upon a Concordat;[1] and seems to favour the idea of a religious establishment—in this country, the Church of England.[2]

Mr Eliot's argument is intricate and I am not sure that I have altogether grasped it, perhaps because some of the steps in the argument have been suppressed. He begins by suggesting that the problem of Church and State 'will take a different form according to the traditions [of the Christian country concerned]—Roman, Orthodox or Lutheran'; and still another form in those countries which have no one predominant religious tradition.[3] This is, of course, true as a matter of sociology. Does it carry with it the implication that the task of the Christian sociologist or political philosopher is to accept the religious tradition of the country in which he happens to be domiciled as a *datum*? Perhaps so; for Mr Eliot restricts himself to the Church of England; seems to suggest—though in its context the sentence is slightly ambiguous—that the Church of England 'can claim to represent the traditional form of Christian belief and worship of the great mass of the people' of this country;[4] and asserts without ambiguity that 'if the idea of a Christian society be grasped and accepted, then it can only be realized, in England, through the Church of England'.[5] Even on the level of history and sociology one might wish to quarrel with this. Many historians would wish to qualify the judgment that Anglicanism does represent the religious tradition of 'the great mass of the people'. There is much to be said for the view that all the English religious traditions are minority traditions, and that the great mass of the people have lived their lives outside these traditions. Hooker's view that Englishman and Anglican are interchangeable terms was no more than a legal fiction when he put it forward and has certainly not acquired any more reality since the end of the Sixteenth Century. The view that only through the Church of England can a Christian society be established in England is a matter of opinion; and no evidence is offered in

[1] *Ibid.*, p. 26. [2] *Ibid.*, p. 46. [3] *Ibid.*, p. 45. [4] *Ibid.*, p. 46. [5] *Ibid.*, p. 47.

support of this—to many Roman Catholic and Protestant dissenters—surprising assertion.

One might wish respectfully to suggest that Mr Eliot is mixing his categories. A Christian society, in the sense in which Mr Eliot wishes to use the term, is a theological and not a sociological category. This is made plain by what he has to say later about the 'increasing recognition of the supranational Christian society' (by oecumenical conferences); and his argument that 'no one today can defend the idea of a National Church, without balancing it with the idea of the Universal Church, and without keeping in mind that truth is one and that theology has no frontiers'.[1] Precisely. And in some fine pages on the need in our society for 'a *respect* for the religious life, for the life of prayer and contemplation' he tells us that 'I should not like the "Community of Christians" of which I have spoken, to be thought of as merely the nicest, most intelligent and public-spirited of the upper middle class—it is not to be conceived on that analogy'.[2]

Now, if the idea of a Christian society is a theological and not a sociological category, it is quite beside the point to consider in any particular country which of the Christian bodies is by reason of history and national prejudice in the best strategic situation. This would be a Latitudinarian position, not unlike that of Dr Arnold. Mr Eliot is certainly not a Latitudinarian. The life of the Christian society is nourished by Grace; and while it would be blasphemous to set limits to the freedom of the Spirit, poured out far beyond the frontiers of Christendom, only on a Latitudinarian theory is it a matter of comparative indifference which institution of all those which claim to be in some sense orthodox churches is to be taken as the *datum*. Of course, in a passage to which I have already referred, Mr Eliot refers to the Universal Church and to 'the supranational Christian society'; but these are (in the sense which they must be given by an Anglican writer) speculative ideas, hopes for an unspecified future, or, at best, spiritual realities without, as yet, any institutional embodiment. It is true, he writes that 'the allegiance of the individual to his own Church is secondary to his allegiance

[1] *Ibid.*, p. 53. [2] *Ibid.*, pp. 60, 61.

to the Universal Church. Unless the National Church is a part of the whole, it has no claim upon me. . . .'[1] Here it is very hard to know in what sense a National Church, an actual institution, is a part of a Universal Church which, on any Anglican theory, has no institutional embodiment, and in what way the allegiance of an individual member of a National Church could show itself.

It is very much a question whether, on any theory of the Church, there is available today any solution better than that of the neutral society on the American model. Mr Eliot is quite right when he says of the solution of the problem of Church and State by means of a Concordat that it is 'a kind of compromise, of doubtful durability, resting on a dubious division of authority, and often a popular division of loyalty; a compromise which implies perhaps a hope on the part of the rulers of the State that their rule will outlast Christianity, and a faith on the part of the Church that it will survive any particular form of secular organization'.[2] Nevertheless, it is also true that a concordatory régime does at least preserve the indispensable distinction between Church and State, the things of God and the things of Caesar; that it does witness, in Mr Eliot's own phrase, to 'a faith on the part of the Church that it will survive any particular form of secular organization'; whereas the defect of an Establishment is that Church and State are so mingled that the necessary distinctions are lost. As Mr Eliot himself puts it in a striking phrase, 'bishops are a part of English culture, and horses and dogs a part of English religion'.[3]

Mr Eliot is so important and so stimulating a writer that a mainly critical treatment of his writings on the range of topics here considered needs no apology. Whatever the defects of that eccentricity to English styles of thinking which I remarked upon earlier, it has the great advantage that it has done much to mitigate the crudity and provincialism of so much English writing on questions of religion, culture and politics. The gaps and ambiguities in his presentation of his themes are from one standpoint virtues rather than vices. Nothing is so unsatisfactory and nothing wears so badly as that

[1] *Ibid.*, p. 54. [2] *Ibid.*, p. 26.
[3] *Notes Towards the Definition of Culture*, p. 32.

logical rigour which springs from a mania for systematization. In dealing with those 'mixed' questions where the problems of religion, culture and politics run together, the *method* employed by Mr Eliot —the examination of particular questions in the light of general principles not too narrowly defined and not too inflexibly stated— is certainly the right one; and it is in my view clear that Mr Eliot's expertness in the use of this method has grown with time. *The Idea of a Christian Society* is a notable advance upon *After Strange Gods*; and *Notes Towards the Definition of Culture* is so much the finest of the works in this vein that the comparison to *Culture and Anarchy* is irresistible; and the comparison is perhaps in Mr Eliot's favour. What, for example, could be finer than this interpretation of totalitarianism?

> The identity of religion and culture remains on the unconscious level, upon which we have superimposed a conscious structure wherein religion and culture are contrasted and can be opposed. The *meaning* of the terms 'religion' and 'culture' is of course altered between these two levels. To the unconscious level we constantly tend to revert, as we find consciousness an excessive burden; and the tendency towards reversion may explain the powerful attraction which totalitarian philosophy and practice can exert upon humanity. Totalitarianism appeals to the desire to return to the womb. The contrast between religion and culture imposes a strain: we escape from this strain by attempting to revert to an identity of religion and culture which prevailed at a more primitive stage; as when we indulge in alcohol as an anodyne, we consciously seek unconsciousness. It is only by unremitting effort that we can persist in being individuals in a society instead of merely members of a disciplined crowd. Yet we remain members of the crowd, even when we succeed in being individuals.[1]

And the following characterization of the English religious situation makes his earlier writing on the same topic seem by contrast doctrinaire.

> In England, as in other Protestant countries, atheism has been mostly of a passive kind. . . . Many people live on an unmarked frontier enveloped in dense fog; and those who dwell beyond it are more numerous in the dark waste of ignorance and indifference than in the well-lighted desert of atheism. The English unbeliever, of some social status however

[1] *Ibid.*, p. 68.

humble, is likely to conform to the practices of Christianity on the occasions of birth, death and the first venture in matrimony. Atheists in this country are not yet culturally united: their types of atheism will vary according to the culture of the religious communion in which they, or their parents, or their grandparents were reared. The chief cultural differences in England have, in the past, been those between Anglicanism and the more important Protestant sects; and even these differences are far from clearly defined: first, because the Church of England itself has comprehended wider variations of belief and cult than a foreign observer would believe it possible for one institution to contain without bursting; and second, because of the number and variety of the sects separated from it.[1]

If—putting aside questions of philosophical and aesthetic criticism—one were asked to say what it is in Mr Eliot's work that speaks to our time of what our time needs, quite apart from any guesses we may have as to whether or not our time will heed him, one might say this: he has kept steadily before us man's dependence upon and hunger for the Absolute; and his capacity for the Eternal. In a shabby and murderous age he has spoken to many who would never be found beneath the pulpits; and to those—all of us—who find ourselves

where is no secure foothold,
And menaced by monsters, fancy lights,
Risking enchantment.

All will salute the achievement of the poet and the critic. It is desirable also to consider the body of thought from which the work of the poet and critic draws its strength. Many will no doubt find it acrid. They should consider whether the fault is in the medicine or in their own palates.

[1] *Ibid.*, pp. 72, 73.

T. S. Eliot as a Moralist

IRIS MURDOCH

A GREAT literary critic can be a most influential moralist; and in this role Mr Eliot has been one of our more important moralists. He has influenced us most, and to an extent which is not at once apparent, so deeply have his lessons been taken to heart, in his less obviously didactic critical writings, wherein he has with some success attempted to reintroduce certain kinds of moral standards into literary criticism. He has also written a considerable number of 'pamphlets', more immediately edifying in their purpose, and as editor of the *Criterion* he constituted himself over many years a close commentator upon his times. 'In one's prose reflections one may be legitimately occupied with ideals, whereas in the writing of verse one can only deal with actuality.'[1] In an age when an exaggerated respect for technicians and experts has silenced many voices, Mr Eliot has been one of the few authoritative persons to continue to utter bold and simple counsels and to draw attention, in politics, to general principles. I shall in what follows be most immediately concerned with these simpler pronouncements uttered 'for edification'; but in order to understand them it will be necessary to pursue Mr Eliot's themes into his more strictly critical writings also.

How can one be a moralist in this age? What does one appeal to? To appreciate the nature of Mr Eliot's moral appeal it is necessary to see the basis of his opposition to 'liberalism'. This exercise is the more valuable since it is surely of the greatest importance for any of us in these days to examine what we take this concept to be. Mr Eliot sees liberalism as the end product of a line of thought which is to be found in Stoicism, in the Renaissance, in Puritanism, in the Romantic Movement and in nineteenth-century Humanism. Characteristic of

[1] *After Strange Gods*, p. 28.

this line of thought is a cult of personality and a denial of authority external to the individual. In the fissure between Dante and Shakespeare lies the loss which Mr Eliot mourns; the self-dramatization of Shakespeare's heroes foreshadows the romanticism of the modern world. The Puritans continued more insidiously to undermine tradition and authority, and with their 'thin mythology' inaugurate the age of amateur religions. Authorized by Kant,[1] inspired by Blake,[2] and more recently encouraged by Huxley, Russell, Wells and others, every man may now invent his own religion, and have the pleasures of religious emotion without the burdens of obedience or dogma. To Puritan influence, too, Mr Eliot (acknowledging a debt to Tawney) traces much of the materialism of our modern industrial society with its worship of 'success'. He himself remembers the morality in which 'it was tacitly assumed that if one was thrifty, enterprising, intelligent, practical and prudent in not violating social conventions, one ought to have a happy and "successful" life'.[3] Romanticism, that debilitated Renaissance, with its denial of original sin and its doctrine of human perfectability, attacking an organism weakened already by the Puritans, produces the new style of emotional individualism; and Humanism, in an attempt at remedy, confounds the categories even further by offering a high-minded version of that confusion of art with religion which with the Romantics had at least remained at a more orgiastic level. So, out of Matthew Arnold, out of the 'dream world' of late romantic poetry, out of the mid-Nineteenth Century, that 'age of progressive degradation',[4] issues liberalism, the imprecise philosophy of a society of materialistic and irresponsible individuals.

Mr Eliot's writings lack the note of tiresome messianism which we find, for instance, in T. E. Hulme; but there is no doubt that he presents us with a picture of a humanity 'fallen' or 'divided' or 'alienated' (to use the Hegelian term which seems oddly apt here) in certain respects, and equally that he has his own positive conception, and

[1] *The Use of Poetry and the Use of Criticism*, p. 135.
[2] *Selected Essays*, p. 321. Essay on 'William Blake'.
[3] Preface to Djuna Barnes's *Nightwood*, p. 6.
[4] *Selected Essays*, p. 427. Essay on 'Baudelaire'.

one which informs his critical writings, of that unity which has been lost and is again to be won. Art should not be 'the expression of personality'. 'The progress of an artist is a continual self-sacrifice, a continual extinction of personality.'[1] The sermons of Andrewes are superior to those of Donne because the emotion of Andrewes 'is not personal'. 'Donne is a "personality" in a sense in which Andrewes is not: his sermons, one feels, are a means of "self-expression". He is constantly finding an object which shall be adequate to his feelings; Andrewes is wholly absorbed in the object and therefore responds with the adequate emotion.'[2] Some time in the Seventeenth Century poets lost the capacity for 'direct sensuous apprehension of thought'. They no longer 'felt their thoughts as immediately as the odour of a rose'.[3] Sensibility was dissociated, emotion parted company with thought and broke loose on its own. Romanticism encouraged its undisciplined expression, and as men lost their sense of limit, poetry lost its 'hardness'. It was Baudelaire, that true blasphemer and believer in sin, that was 'the first counter-romantic in poetry',[4] and one of the initiators of the movement, which we connect with Imagism and notably with Mr Eliot, which attempts to reintroduce 'precise emotion' and to draw the artist's attention 'back to the object'. This putting of emotion in its place is at the same time a putting of poetry in its place. Poetry cannot play the part of religion. The more we realize what literature is, and what it *cannot* do, the more we return soberly to a sense of our own limitations. Baudelaire, Mr Eliot says, would surely have approved of these words of T. E. Hulme: man

> is endowed with original sin. While he can occasionally accomplish acts which partake of perfection, he can never himself *be* perfect. Certain secondary results in regard to ordinary human action in society follow from this. A man is essentially bad, he can only accomplish anything of value by discipline—ethical and political. Order is thus not merely negative, but creative and liberating. Institutions are necessary.[5]

[1] *Selected Essays*, p. 17. Essay on 'Tradition and the Individual Talent'.
[2] *Ibid.*, p. 351. Essay on 'Launcelot Andrewes'.
[3] *Ibid.*, p. 287. Essay on 'The Metaphysical Poets'.
[4] *Ibid.*, p. 424. Essay on 'Baudelaire'.
[5] *Ibid.*, p. 430. Essay on 'Baudelaire'.

I give merely a sketch of what is clearly a profoundly unified attitude whose 'literary' faces have 'metaphysical' faces to correspond. (This unity of Mr Eliot's attitude is also my excuse for treating as one 'position' utterances made over a number of years.) 'Dissociation of sensibility' serves as a symbol for Mr Eliot of the loss, in some far more general sense, of a unified world: the loss of a sense of limit and of an understanding of where each thing has its place. The limiting and rendering precise of emotion is one aspect of the criticism of the messy and uninhibited 'liberal individual'. Liberalism, then, destroys tradition through challenging authority. In a society where every man's opinion is equally valuable there is no unity of outlook. This favours over-specialization, the worship of techniques, and the division of one part of society from another. Liberalism is a creed which dissipates and relaxes; and it 'prepares the way for that which is its own negation: the artificial, mechanized or brutalized control which is a desperate remedy for its chaos'.[1] We have the choice of a society bound for the extremes of paganism, or a society more positively Christian than our own. Mr Eliot turns to appeal, over the head of the dominant creed of the time, to an older, purer tradition. The historical reality upon which he relies is the Anglican Church, the only instrument through which the conversion of England can be achieved; and he pictures a Christian society, inspired by a Christian élite, and reminded by the Church of standards which lie beyond the individual.

There is a revolution of our time and a 'new sensibility', in the creation of which Mr Eliot has played a major part; and before going on to consider his morals and politics more closely let us look for a moment at this scene of change. G. E. Moore, the father of modern philosophy, and incidentally a thinker hailed with approval by Hulme, placed as epigraph to his *Principia Ethica* the words of Butler: 'everything is what it is and not another thing'; and when Mr Eliot himself remarks (*à propos* of poetry and religion) that 'nothing in this world or the next is a substitute for anything else'[2] he speaks with the voice of the age. We have become increasingly,

[1] *The Idea of a Christian Society*, p. 16.
[2] *The Use of Poetry and the Use of Criticism*, p. 113.

sometimes excessively, self-conscious about our concepts and our language, and anxious to delimit categories and prevent the spilling over of one thing into another. Mr Eliot's is not the only eye which looks upon the Nineteenth Century as an era of messy thinking, and one can readily parallel, in other disciplines, his exasperated cry, 'Arnold does not see what poetry *is*'. Science, philosophy, history, criticism have become more specialized, more acutely conscious of their own limitations. Mr Eliot, too, is, in this respect, exemplary. He has carried, one wants to say with a sort of 'heroism', his self-awareness about language into the depths of his poetry, into 'the intolerable wrestle with words and meanings' and the attack upon 'the general mess of imprecision of feeling'. Unlike some other poets in the Imagist tradition, Mr Eliot has never lost his respect for words. The desire, as Hulme put it, to 'hand over sensations bodily'[1] has never led Mr Eliot to make war upon language after the manner of Mallarmé or Pound. One of the deep characteristics of his poetry is a continual concern, in the midst of difficulties, for the referential character of words. (This one most movingly feels in the *Four Quartets*.) As a prose writer equally Mr Eliot has shown an exemplary sense of the limitations of his job. He does not trespass upon the field of technical philosophy, but says what he has to say, as critic and as moralist, precisely and appropriately. He is aware, and shares this concern with certain contemporary moral philosophers,[2] that a deterioration in morals is a destruction of concepts. If our convictions part company with our vocabulary of justification, our controversies become empty. 'We are living at present in a kind of doldrums between opposing winds of doctrine, in a period in which one political philosophy has lost its cogency, though it is still the only one in which public speech can be framed. This is very bad for the English language. . . . Good prose cannot be written by people without convictions.'[3] In these ways, Mr Eliot is not alone, but belongs with other makers of his age. He is the great poet of the new sensibility, one aspect of which is categorical precision, while the

[1] *Speculations*, p. 134.
[2] See, for instance, R. M. Hare's *The Language of Morals*.
[3] *The Idea of a Christian Society*, pp. 19–20.

other aspect is what Hulme called 'cinders' and Sartre called '*nausée*'. 'The return to the object' has its unnerving moments. 'It is essential to prove that beauty may be in small dry things,' said Hulme. 'The great aim is accurate, precise description. The first thing is to recognize how extraordinarily difficult this is.'[1] One is reminded of the hard, dry, piecemeal character of the philosophy of Wittgenstein. For precise description reveals to the unillusioned gaze a world reduced to pieces: 'Men and bits of paper, whirled by the cold wind.' The synthesis of the Nineteenth Century, that premature and shallow integration, is no longer available to us. To what can we appeal?

Mr Eliot, it seems, is very much a member of our age; but with the zeal of a 'rationalist', using that word in its popular sense, he tends to attribute his insights to the Christian tradition, narrowly considered, while he collects the contemporary vices together under the name of liberalism. In spite of his appreciation of compromise-making Anglicanism, that 'uneasy bed', Mr Eliot is more fundamentally an anti-Puritan Puritan, invoking the evil-conscious Puritanism of Hawthorne and James against the 'decayed Protestantism' of the present, in which he sees on one hand the materialism analysed by Tawney, and on the other the 'dreary hymn-singing pietism' which he attributes to D. H. Lawrence's mother. He speaks of those 'vast hosts of the dead' of whose presence James Joyce was aware; but the dead whom the political Mr Eliot venerates lie far away. Mr Eliot is notably not in the English conservative tradition. He is an eclectic moralist. One feels that the voice of Krishna, bidding us not to think of the fruit of action, rings more loudly in his ears; whereas he is less patient with that medley of voices, to which T. H. Greene, for instance, lent careful attention, which constitutes the English political creed. He praises Bradley, who is 'wise', whose philosophy (unlike that of his successors) is 'catholic, civilized and universal', and who destroyed, more surely than Arnold, the bases of contemporary Benthamism. But Mr Eliot's own political and philosophical understanding is remote from the flexible and concrete thinking of the Idealists. One finds in him something of that 'Jansenism of tem-

[1] *Speculations*, pp. 131–2.

perament' which he attributes to Pascal: Mr Eliot, with his dislike of 'untidy lives', being perhaps also one 'who cannot avoid seeing through human beings and observing the vanity of their thoughts and of their avocations, their dishonesty and self-deception, the insincerity of their emotions, their cowardice, the pettiness of their real ambitions'.[1] One feels this disillusioned tone in Mr Eliot's political writings, especially in his attitude to 'the mob'. He declares, alarmingly, that he would prefer an illiterate audience to an audience of ill-educated or half-educated persons such as are now available.[2] And it is significant that he extends no sympathy to the English Nonconformist tradition, with its wide-reaching utilitarian and socialist connections. When Methodism receives a kind word in the book on 'Culture' it is partly because it helped to pave the way for the Oxford Movement.

With hair-raising thoroughness Mr Eliot rejects the 'stuff' of our liberal world. I find something instructive here in his attitude to certain novelists. He gives approval to Jane Austen, Dickens and Thackeray, because with them 'personality . . . was more nearly in its proper place. The standards by which they criticized their world, if not very lofty ones, were at least not of their own making'. But George Eliot unfortunately combined her profounder insights with 'the dreary rationalism of the epoch' and is 'of the same tribe as all the serious and eccentric moralists we have had since',[3] and whom Mr Eliot deplores. But it is in D. H. Lawrence that the extremity is reached of heretical belief and unrestrained and morbid emotionalism. Mr Eliot finds in Lawrence 'a lack not so much of information as of the critical faculties which education should give, and an incapacity for what we ordinarily call thinking'.[4] This is an astonishing judgment. Whatever *is* thinking if Lawrence couldn't think; and what is serious moral reflection if George Eliot, whatever her beliefs, does not present a most lofty instance of it? I think that this is more than a verbal question, and I would connect it, very cautiously, with some of Mr Eliot's views on Shakespeare. Mr Eliot

[1] *Selected Essays*, p. 414. Essay on 'The Pensées of Pascal'.
[2] *The Use of Poetry and the Use of Criticism*, p. 152.
[3] *After Strange Gods*, pp. 53–4.
[4] *Ibid.*, p. 58.

says that 'neither Shakespeare nor Dante did any real thinking', but 'it happened that at Dante's time thought was orderly and strong and beautiful' and so 'Dante's poetry receives a boost'.[1] Shakespeare is also compared unfavourably as a 'thinker' with Marlowe. I suspect that what lies behind these uses of language is a somewhat abstract and mathematical model of thinking ('orderly, strong and beautiful') which one may connect with medieval Christianity and Thomist metaphysics. And one might suggest in reply that our mixed-up modern world needs for its unravelling a type of sensitive 'concrete' understanding to which if we deny the name of thinking we are lost. But these are only hints and guesses.

Mr Eliot has rightly said that it is important in what *terms* a justification is framed. (Pagan statesmen may be 'contained' by the Christian ethos of their people: only certain justifications will serve.)[2] It is especially important now to keep alive such sources of moral response as remain to us. It seems to me that Mr Eliot plays dangerously when he rejects *in toto* the moral content of liberalism and appeals over its head to a conception of dogma and authority which can itself play an ambivalent role. In 1933 Mr Eliot remarked that 'it was better to worship a Golden Calf than to worship nothing'.[3] And in 1939 he said that we should object to fascism because it is pagan. Objections to oppression and cruelty are 'objections to means not to ends'. In fact, the ordinary person dislikes fascism 'because he is fearful of authority'.[4] To argue in this way is to belittle that naked respect for the human person as such which one may connect with Locke and with Kant, and which one hopes has become a part of the English political tradition. Can this be set aside as a romantic over-valuation of the individual? It is at least perilous to neglect the remnants of that liberal moral absolutism which, without dogma, holds that there are certain things which cannot be done to human persons. It is to such a remnant of liberal faith that a book such as P. H. Simon's *Contre La Torture* is addressed, and has perhaps not altogether failed. It may be added that John Stuart Mill, that argu-

[1] *Selected Essays*, p. 136. Essay on 'Shakespeare and the Stoicism of Seneca'.
[2] *The Idea of a Christian Society*, pp. 27–8.
[3] *Criterion*, April 1933.
[4] *The Idea of a Christian Society*, pp. 20, 70.

mentative and undogmatic absolutist, was not merely 'a Romantic', but was remotely a maker, too, of that dry and critical atmosphere in which Mr Eliot among others has flourished.

Mr Eliot may reply that morality must be based on *truth*, and that he is more concerned with the promulgation of truth than with the cultivation of benevolent impulses resting on misunderstandings. It may be that the Christian tradition must be the salvation of the West; but to argue this too narrowly is to neglect aspects of liberalism which are, to put it mildly, worth preserving, and to neglect, too, the extent to which liberalism is entwined with our Christian tradition as it in reality and as a working power now is. We may agree profoundly with many of Mr Eliot's indictments of present-day society, and agree with him, for instance, when he says that the events of September 1938 inspired in him 'a doubt of the validity of civilization'.[1] And there are events since then which inspire similar doubts. But whatever our religious beliefs, we must hope that the liberal world can regenerate itself out of its own resources—and we must seek the Christian tradition, in its various forms, within that world. I would agree with F. R. Leavis who, in defending D. H. Lawrence against Mr Eliot, said, 'It is characteristic of the world as it is that health cannot anywhere be found whole'; and added that 'the sense in which Lawrence stands for health is an important one'.[2] We cannot now afford to squander any of our 'health', which must be sought, with discrimination, in many quarters; and to say this is, of course, to take up a liberal attitude.

At the last word, however, one must return to Mr Eliot the poet. Mr Eliot observed that 'the essential advantage for a poet is not to have a beautiful world with which to deal: it is to be able to see beneath both beauty and ugliness; to see the boredom and the horror and the glory'.[3] Mr Eliot has seen, and it is a great part of our 'health' that we have a poet who can penetrate our anxious trivial world with such a profound compassion. In his poetry Mr Eliot is no Jansenist. We need thus to be helped to 'imagine that which we know': and to say this is, of course, to take up a Romantic attitude.

[1] *Ibid.*, p. 64. [2] *The Common Pursuit*, pp. 246–7.
[3] *The Use of Poetry and the Use of Criticism*, p. 106.

T. S. Eliot as a Contemplative Poet

RAYMOND PRESTON

I HAVE spent many hours in company with T. S. Eliot, but only one hour actually face to face with him. It would therefore seem mistaken to attach any special significance to this one hour, but for the fact that it strikingly confirmed certain impressions that I had gained from the others. It took place, in 1951, on St Lucy's Day; though this may have been merely a happy accident. I remember making only one direct reference to his work, and that was in relating an experience of the Good Friday poem in *East Coker* which seemed to interest and please him particularly. It evidently corresponded to certain experiences of his own. I was travelling by train. I was more than usually tired; but I found myself recalling the lines of *East Coker* with that peculiar detachment and clarity which the motion of a journey can sometimes induce. And I found myself perceiving the different meanings of those lines with a vividness and simultaneity which has not since been repeated. He then said, in answer to some question of mine about the use of poetry for meditation, that in composing that passage he was occupied with the craftsman's problems (and here, in his manner, and in the movement of his fingers as on the typewriter, he conveyed to me the extreme absorption and labour of composition); he then added that he thought they were probably influenced by the practice of the rosary and in particular by the Sorrowful Mysteries.

The chief subject of our conversation was the contemplative life. He expressed the view, which I should have expected of him, though I did not remember reading any direct statement, that it was for each of us to discover that degree of contemplative 'withdrawal' which he needed in order to give the 'maximum potency to his action'; and that such withdrawal was not escape. If some of us found ourselves going into religious communities and remaining there, we were all 'in the same boat'; and each of us, trying to work out his own vocation, 'generally falls short'.

I think that this last was the most significant note of our interview; but only in complement with another. The most definite memory I have of the meeting was of a personality and impersonality together which gave a special emphasis to what he said which no report can suggest. There was a sense of inadequacy and inarticulacy that was even painful; there were statements which seemed to come *through* him as if through a mask, with an effect of surprise and even frightening power. I was aware of a man capable of assuming different *personae* (I do not mean vulgarly 'playing various parts'): including, as in *The Waste Land*, the *persona* of the prophet. I was aware of a man capable of coming to the point of despair about himself, and of carrying on—carrying on long enough and persistently enough to discover power beyond himself. I was aware of a contemplative.

I have said that this meeting strikingly confirmed certain impressions of his work. I should state also that these impressions have been confirmed, on the other side, by the accident of returning to T. S. Eliot after a very different experience. Since publishing an essay called '*Four Quartets*' *Rehearsed* in 1946 I have written about an author who is a strong candidate for the title of the greatest comedian-poet of Christendom. It would be difficult to think of anything more likely to change my view of T. S. Eliot than four or five years of frequenting the work of Geoffrey Chaucer. It is not that I imagine Mr Eliot without a sense of comedy; on the contrary, I think a sense of comedy has been his saving grace at several points; especially in his early poems. Anyone who is inclined to take the *Love Song of J. Alfred Prufrock* with solemnity should hear a recording which exists of Mr Eliot reading that poem in the Library of Congress. It is the best performance of Mr Eliot's that has come my way. In the stony silence, broken only by asthmatic coughing of his audience, you can hear that without prejudice to the clarity of his diction Mr Eliot's tongue is quite beautifully in his cheek. Either the Librarians of Congress are singularly deficient in a sense of humour, or none of them dared to laugh, that is all. Failing a prolonged reading of a very great comedian, I can only suggest, to anyone who wishes to read the work of T. S. Eliot with greater detachment, repetition of this recording.

That the *Love Song of J. Alfred Prufrock* is a fine comic poem is, I believe, its essential quality, and the quality that most of us who began to read T. S. Eliot as adolescents almost completely missed. The adolescent in his most serious moments is so painfully imprisoned in his own frustrations and constraints and sense of impotence that he cannot conceive the possibility of seeing them, by an act of will, from the outside. The difficulty is not only a difficulty of adolescence. Mr Eliot has written in his own way on this very matter. He has spoken of the poet's problem of finding a subject which offers him *the deepest and most secret release.* Now the release of the deepest tensions and desires is the cause of unaccountable personal preferences for certain works of art. These personal preferences may add up to a formidable consensus of opinion, and even, over a considerable period of time, to an accepted judgment; and it is for the poet, as for the reader, to discover how far he is merely eccentric.

This is part of my larger theme, which you may find suggested by the first image in *Collected Poems 1909–35.* This once notorious opening has reminded me of Donne:

> Whilst my Physitians by their love are growne
> Cosmographers, and I their Mappe who lie
> Flat on this bed

or of other early versions of 'The whole earth is our hospital'; or on the other hand of the hymn in the Office of None, which prays for a glorious evening in death. All these things have very different meanings, meanings as different as the word of my theme, which is despair. If we say that this is an age of despair and anxiety, and that Mr Eliot, without being anxious, is a very good poet of despair, we are not likely to be contradicted: but we may be asked for a definition. And it is definition which will bring new meaning to an apparently commonplace statement. Here is a word which can mean either death or life. If despair is a suicidal anguish, it is not necessarily leading to suicide. Despair is a stage in going back, or going forward. At one extreme it is the sin against the Holy Ghost: at the other it is a term St Gregory of Nyssa used for that inner tension which is a beginning for the contemplative. There is the despair which is evil, and may be the ultimate evil; and there is the despair which is a stage in advance, in any real progress. And at certain points, from the outside, they are difficult to tell apart: like the detachment and indifference defined in *Little Gidding*. They may be difficult to tell apart even from the inside, so that the saint, on the last lap, thinks he is lost, or the knight nearing the Chapel Perilous is utterly desolate, 'menaced by monsters', by 'voices of temptation', by hallucinations, by the 'disconsolate chimera'.

Drought, dryness, is the condition of despair in the mystic or the contemplative, and by analogy in the poet or musician or artist, in any maker. You have the two together, mystic and maker, as long ago as David, in the psalms: the desert, the dry land, the thirsty land—the Waste Land—of Old Testament poetry and prophecy, at a beginning of all the mystics' symbolism. And the poet or musician or any good craftsman (*il miglior fabbro*) can imagine this experience, even if he is not himself a mystic: for he knows that time of hopelessness, of darkness when everything seems to be going wrong, but when, in fact (if he only knew it—or rather, if he could only know that it is a good thing that he doesn't know it), everything is going right.

Coming to T. S. Eliot afresh from the medieval serenity of Chaucer on the one hand and of the fourteenth-century mystics on the other, I find this problem of despair at the centre of the work of T. S. Eliot and of first importance for our own age. As I have suggested, it is a matter of release from self: from the comic projection of everyday frustrations into the middle-aged Prufrock, in and out of a rarified drawing-room: to *datta, dayadhvam, damyata* of *The Waste Land*: and beyond. *The Waste Land* was the farthest that he could reach without giving himself up wholly to a dive in the dark: let us say the farthest that we could reach. And *The Hollow Men* is there to show how desperately we needed, or still need, to make the leap. *We are the hollow men. Ash-Wednesday* is a poem of turning: when you do not know which way to turn, you turn, you strive in every way to the limit of your strength, until you give way: then there is nothing left but to wait to *be turned.* (*Turn us then. . . . Wilt thou not turn again and quicken us?*)

> Because I do not hope to turn again . . .
>
> Teach us to care and not to care
> Teach us to sit still.

It is a poem of the 'time of tension between dying and birth'. And that is the condition—very painful, like healing—of the good despair of St Gregory of Nyssa: the tension between two forces, one seeming to lead up, and the other down, dejection wanting to be exalted, and elation needing to be humbled. And the 'way up' and the 'way down', in the terms of Heraclitus, are the two musical subjects, the two principal themes, of *Four Quartets.*

They are, says Heraclitus, 'one and the same': and this is as difficult to understand at once as to understand that we are talking about one and the same poet who wrote about death, and time and the sea in the *Love Song of J. Alfred Prufrock*. The same symbols and words have been turned, as the poet has been turned, turned and broken and renewed, until they have made new meanings.

> We have lingered in the chambers of the sea

and

> The notion of some infinitely gentle
> Infinitely suffering thing

and

> And indeed there will be time . . .
> To prepare a face for the faces that you meet;
> There will be time to murder and create . . .
> Time for you and time for me . . .

and

> Well! and what if she should die some afternoon . . .

—those lines so reminiscent of Baudelaire at the end of the earliest poem in the collected volume: all these seem to have *grown* since we first read them, and in ways we did not guess.

'And now that we talk of dying', you will remember that Mr Eliot has always found it useful to project himself some way forward in time, whether in Prufrock, or Gerontion, or the agèd eagle, or the familiar compound ghost.

But I must go back and explain what I meant by the two *musical* subjects of *Four Quartets*. It is curious that Mr Eliot's finest lyrical poems are so rarely performed. (It is perhaps even more curious that Mr Eliot's most dramatic poem, *The Waste Land*, is hardly ever performed either.) For we cannot be said to have looked through *Four Quartets* with any sensitiveness unless we want to read them aloud, or to hear them read aloud, or are interested in different ways of performing them. The interpretation of *Four Quartets* ought not to mean merely the laborious and clumsy business of making a commentary upon them: it ought to include those shades of meaning which can only be properly conveyed by a particular emphasis or tone of the voice. For this reason we are fortunate to have Mr Eliot's recording: not because (as he himself was the first to point out) his emphases or tones are the only possible ones, or the best, but because he does demonstrate, particularly in his rendering of the vision in the rose-garden of Burnt Norton and of the sea voyage in the *Dry Salvages*, something of what 'interpretation' of his poetry ought to mean—something without which any amount of writing about it is a waste of time. The quality of T. S. Eliot's work has always been at once perceptible in what he likes to call 'music', even in incantation: in that movement of language which allows for the release of forces deeper than we are ordinarily conscious of, or prolongs our naturally limited capacity for meditation. Now Mr Eliot has suggested what we can in any case guess from his practice, that a theme forms itself in his mind not directly, but in what he calls 'fragments of musical rhythm'. These are the beginnings of a poem. Those readers who are in a hurry to find the meaning must remember that the poet was trying to find it, too: and that the poet will think himself lucky if he comes to the point at which he can thankfully give up the attempt, having constructed something that shall first of all *be*, that can stand; whatever, within a certain controlled range, it turns out to 'mean'. Add that his ambition is, in his own words, to 'get beyond poetry'; and that poetry is a way of travelling without short-cuts, vehicles or guide-books to a destination which you do not quite know till you get there; and the completed act of the journey is what matters. Transported by the usual means, you are still a potential traveller at the end. You are persuaded that you have arrived before you really know what it means to start. So much, at least, the experience of the poetry conveys.

What then are these germinative phrases, these fragments of musical rhythm, that set the poem going? I think that one of them is apparent from the emphasis of Mr Eliot's own reading of the first and third movements of *Burnt Norton.* The particular beat I have in mind is simply the insistent emphasis on the word *Time*: the rhythm of futile endless repetition: time before and time after, but never NOW. It is the 'ridiculous waste sad time' of the fifth movement, and a slightly different variation of a beat that seems to have been a part of the poet's nervous system from *Prufrock* onwards. This is the rhythm that goes to form, or propels, what I shall call the first theme of *Four Quartets*: 'time before and time after'.

The second rhythmic fragment which I take to be an essential germinative phrase comes first, so far as I remember, in a little piece called 'Cape Ann':

> O quick quick quick, quick hear the song-sparrow . . .

It is suggested by the darting of a bird or a sudden rapid twittering. You can hear it at the beginning of *Burnt Norton*:

> Quick, said the bird, find them, find them,
> Round the corner.

And by the end of this first poem it is established as a *motif* to which the whole sequence can return.

This second theme of *Four Quartets—Quick now, here, here, now, always . . .*—contains the meaning of the present moment. It is a musical phrase corresponding to the trilling wire in the blood, the moment in the rose-garden, the winter lightning, the laughter in the garden, the sudden illumination. . . .

These are, in musical terms, the two principal themes of *Four Quartets*: one negative, the other positive. The one is the endless conveyor-belt of time, boredom and horror, futility, the laceration of laughter at what ceases to amuse, meaningless (in the *Dry Salvages* he writes of striving for the meaning and seems to hang on desperately to the word): distracted from distraction by distraction . . . the vacant into the vacant. . . . This is the despair of the 'way down'. And this theme, we remember, is insistent in Eliot's early work—even, when he first 'arrived', characteristic. What is new in the later work, in *Ash-Wednesday* and *Four Quartets*, is the way it changes inevitably—not through any hopes or contrivings or tinkerings of the poet—to show a way out of the horror. The poet is not turning the theme, is not setting out to try and cheer us up; he and the theme are *being turned*, we are being cheered when we can see no hope whatever. (The theological virtue of Hope has nothing whatever to do with being hearty; it is much more like the kernel breaking out of the husk.) We can find that happening again, astonishingly, in the at first apparently infernal second part of *Little Gidding*. What is new is the complete emergence, and complete acceptance—there is no question of insertion—of the positive second theme, of the 'moments of happiness' when there *is* meaning, of the 'way up'.

We have advanced from the small fragment of rhythm in words, the little musical phrase that is conceivably the poet's beginning, to the theme felt and established for a whole musical cycle, a whole sequence of poems. There is a further stage: the theme becoming *idea*. So the first theme leads to discursive passages on the time process; and the second to the *timeless moment*, and to the very word *Incarnation*, the reality of which, it may relevantly be said, is what makes the poetry possible. I can only assume that when certain otherwise sensitive readers (of whom the most sensitive is probably Dr F. R. Leavis) ignore or discount these abstract passages, they are in effect accepting a notion of T. S. Eliot's technique which may be in some respects critically more rigorous than certain other notions, but which is incomplete. It simply does not correspond to the facts. Whether these facts in the poem are *articles of faith* for the reader is, of course, another matter. The possibility of a technique exhibiting as wide a range from concrete to abstract as the technique of *Four Quartets* was demonstrated once and for all by Dante.

But the readers I have mentioned would I believe at once agree with my last observation, which is that the recurring symbols of the sequence—darkness, fire, the rose and the yew-tree, the sea—are means by which our two themes are related. They are all ambiguous symbols, ambiguous as nature, which can be conceived as a plane of meeting of two worlds. All of them show possibilities of natural transition from the one theme to the other, from the 'way down' to the 'way up'. The darkness which we have called despair is also the 'darkness of God'.

History or Poetic Drama?

STEVIE SMITH

Murder in the Cathedral is a remarkable evocation of Christian fears; remarkable for the strength of these fears and the horrible beauty in which they are dressed; remarkable, too, for the religious convictions from which they spring. The year in which it was published was 1935. If this was a godless and frivolous period, frivolity masking the guilt and uncertainty of our western behaviour, and if there was once a better behaviour, running in the churchly times of Mr Eliot's choice, then this play comes like Hamlet's portrait of his father which he shows to Gertrude. Look on this, it says, and reform yourself. The author's purpose is as serious as Hamlet's and as violent. But Hamlet was violent because he was going off his head for worry lest the ghost prove false; Mr Eliot's violence does not always seem so straightforward as this, but rather to be used as a cover for some thoughts that are equivocal, as in the speeches the knights make to justify their murder. In these speeches may be seen all that Mr Eliot believes, and thinks we should believe, about the sickness of states and the lies of statesmen, and the shared guilt of the public, 'living and partly living', who allow smooth-speaking fools and villains to lead them astray. But this does not seem a constructive political opinion, it seems rather childish, as if he thought men did not sometimes have to govern, as if he thought that by the act of governing they became at once not men but monsters. It is a disingenuous and not uncommon thought, it is one aspect of the arrogance of art and the arrogance of highmindedness divorced from power, it is something one should not put up with. But just as Shakespeare's poor Gertrude, who has all the same more spirit than Mr Eliot's people of Canterbury, was struck with swords to the heart when Hamlet showed her the Royal Dane's picture, so audiences and readers of this play are meant to be struck. But what, in fact, is the effect? Uneasiness, I think—to begin with. And not because we are drawn into the guilt of the two sorts of sinners who are depicted here, the sinners who are powerful in action and the sinners who are feeble and small and too frightened to act at all. No, it is the uneasiness of dubiety.

Is this how it was, is this the truth? Is it the truth of history, philosophy, or the Christian religion? Writers do not have to be impartial, as scholars of history are impartial; they may take events and personages of the past and fit them to their uses. The fact that Castlereagh had something to be said for him does not invalidate Shelley's cry against tyranny, or mar the beauty of his poem 'I met Murder on his way, / He had a mask like Castlereagh'. But allowing this freedom in historical interpretation, and misinterpretation, still leaves us the right to ask what a poet is after. Shelley, writing against tyranny, made Castlereagh his villain. Mr Eliot makes Henry and the State his villains, and what is he after? It is something that at first sight looks noble. But is it? Is it not rather something ignoble, a flight from largeness into smallness, a flight in fear to a religion of fear, from freedom to captivity, from human dignity to degradation? For fear is degrading, and we are counselled, for our soul's good, to fear. Is this the truth of philosophy and religion? Back to the Church, he cries, and he makes his archbishop so truly good and strong a man that we may forget to ask, Were they all like this, is the Church so sweet a thing, does it smell so sweet, was it not already, at this time of Becket, a bride of Christ somewhat stained with blood and no less greedy for political power than the State? Becket may or may not have been a man of the cast of Mr Eliot's archbishop. Mr Eliot's dealings with him are permissible, but is it permissible to distort the truths of humanity and offend against them, to cover the needs of men with a meretricious coat, and to envisage with delight a dwindling of hope and courage? There is this beauty in the play that I have called horrible. Seldom has fear worn such colours. Especially we find these rich colours in the chorus: 'What is the sickly smell, the vapour, the dark green light from a cloud on a withered tree? . . . what is the sticky dew that forms on the back of my hand?' 'We have not been happy, my lord, we have not been happy.' This might seem a trifle on the Greek pattern, indeed Mr Eliot uses banality with beauty in the Greek fashion that is so often parodied for an easy joke, e.g. 'I hear cries within the house, all is not well'. But there is nothing Grecian in the temper of this chorus of the women of Canterbury. They are a curious lot. They are really saying all the time 'I am afraid', and with colour and variety they say it, 'I have eaten the living lobster, the crab, the oyster, and they live and spawn in my bowels'. This neurosis of the invasion of uncleanliness and sin enlivens all their crying, 'We are soiled by a filth that we cannot clean, united to supernatural vermin'.

There seems something peculiar to the author in these dreams of corruption entering the body 'like a pattern of living worms in the guts of the women of Canterbury', it is a private horror (and it is communicated), the sort of thing that is so well described, in a naturalist's terms, in Mr Henry Williamson's *Salar the Salmon* and which makes that book such painful reading—a living body entering a living body to feed and live within it and upon it. So to fear must be added disgust. The sense of disgust in the chorus is the most living thing out of all the play. It is splendidly alive, this sense, most often beautiful, only once or twice running near those reefs of silliness which make the waters of disgust dangerous to sailors. The argument of the play seems altogether lighter. It is both theme and purpose, yet it is not strong, as the emotions of fear and disgust are strong, but lies on the surface, an elegant and clever foam. I do not mean he may not believe what he argues, only that he does not make us as sure that he *believes* as he makes us sure that he *feels*, and especially that he feels disgust and enjoys feeling disgust and indulges this feeling with the best of his poetry. Against his arguments may easily be brought counter arguments. Mr Eliot is well aware of this and has put many of these counter arguments into the speeches of his self-justifying murderers. But these counter arguments are valid, for all that they are given a cynical man-of-the-worldliness, the flip and deliberate mannerisms of our own times. It *is* better that law should be one and equal. When the murderers cry to the sheeplike people of Canterbury that however much the King may repudiate their action, the benefits that will arrive from it will be thanks to them, they are not strictly telling the truth. It might be argued that the martyrdom of Becket put back by about 400 years the reforms to which Mr Eliot gives so glib and derogatory a character. Yet the knightly murderers have some true thoughts about these reforms in spite of the cynical way they speak. There is some special pleading in the mannerism of the knights, as there is some special pleading in the absolute nobility of Mr Eliot's Becket. But these knights, in their city-slicker-cum-M.P.-cum-landed-fox dress of modernity, are also for a light relief, I suppose, a sort of joke, no worse than Shaw's seminarist coming in at the end of *St Joan*, no worse and no better. It is not they, and it is not the arguments that lie at the roots of this play, it is fear and horror it beds in and from fear and horror it draws its sap. With a sure touch Mr Eliot touches that Christian nerve which responds so shockingly to fear and cruelty, which Dante touched most surely of all, and one might have hoped for all time. What is this religion that is like a game of snakes and ladders, or a game between a cat and a mouse? Even the saintly Becket is played with in this way. 'Your sin soars heavenward covering king's falcons' cries the tempter, and Becket stands wondering whether pride may not bring even a martyr's crown tumbling to hell. And it is exciting, is it not, it adds savour, a speculation of that sort takes the flatness out of life? One observes how the poetry mounts at each touch of pain and sinks when, as does not often happen, something agreeable comes to mind. The weather and landscapes are most alive when they are ugly: the 'sullen Dover', the rain, the fog and the sleet. Yet Dover, with its great cliffs, and the skirts of its great castle gracefully fanned, is not sullen, the sea lies aroar and the fields arch above. Why did these worm-haunted towns-people never turn their eyes that way? Living in the sweetest landscapes of England, empty then of pylons and pill-boxes, with the sea below them, coloured and aroar, you might have thought they would have looked, as you might have thought the Lord had juster cause to torment them for not looking, than for any cause that Mr Eliot shows. But, of course, he is right; in his own terms he is right. A lifting of hearts for pleasant fields would have broken the gloom, and he did not wish it broken, except in a little way as he breaks it, a little hellish way, by the rattle of the knights' tongues.

One thinks that Mr Eliot believes his terror-talk of cat-and-mouse damnation, and that with him it is not a case of having to have some terror about in order to make things more exciting, as seems sometimes to be the case with his fellow religious terror writers. But it seems curious, condemnable really, that so many writers of these times, which need courage and the power of criticism, and coolness, should find their chief delight in terrifying themselves and their readers with past echoes of cruelty and nonsense, 'pacing for ever' (to use Mr Eliot's words with a different application) 'in the hell of make-believe'. One would not write like this if the play were not so beautiful and strong in its feelings, but it is beautiful and strong in these feelings, and also it is abominable. And this is not to forget the noble beauty of Mr Eliot's Becket and the strains of his situation. There is true love in that man, but it seems to be in spite of his strains and not because of them. And how significant—to show how he turns from love to severity—is the alteration Mr Eliot has made in the film script of his play. It is a disputed biblical text that is altered, but a wise heart would have adhered to our English Bible's rendering.

In the play Mr Eliot uses this rendering, 'on earth peace, good will toward men', but in the film script this becomes 'peace on earth to men of good will', which is a limitation and shrinkage of charity, for all men need good will, and most of all those who do not have it. How curious the Christian conviction sometimes seems! I recall reading in a religious manual on pain that Man's state since the fall is more blessed than it was before, because of the benefits of Christ's sacrifice upon the cross to which he now is heir. Then God must need sin, since without it Man could not have become 'more blessed'? So then, indeed, his good will should be extended to all men, and they should have this good will, yes, they should have it, and the niggling down, which is the sense of the amended text 'to men of good will', should not be allowed. But what is this but a fairy comment on a fairy story, a tribute to an inventiveness that bears the mark of humanity, being so exciting and so fanciful?

Truth is far and flat, and fancy is fiery; and truth is cold, and people feel the cold, and they may wrap themselves against it in fancies that are fiery, but they should not call them facts; and, generally, poets do not; they are shrewd, they feel the cold, too, but they know a hawk from a handsaw, a fact from a fancy, as none knows better. So Mr Eliot's play does not seem to me to be quite plausible, but to be very interesting and to draw one after it. He is a powerful writer and one to pay homage to and be thankful for, he stirs our thoughts and does no harm, if our minds are cool he does no harm but gives pleasure. Not every great writer is so enjoyable, not by a long way.

'Not Much About Gods'

MARTIN JARRETT-KERR, CR

ONE of the most endearing and tantalizing qualities of Mr Eliot's poetry is its humility. Tantalizing, because it sometimes leads to what seems almost like striking an attitude, when the poem keeps taking back what it has managed with great effort to say ('that was one way of putting it'), and so leaves the impression that one can never get further than 'notes towards a definition', notes of notes, a craftsman's sketch-book, and therefore that anyone who attempts more is foolish. But endearing, because, as Dr F. R. Leavis recognized so clearly for us, the *Four Quartets* is the only kind of religious statement that can be validly made in poetry today. And I take it that the concentration in the *Four Quartets* upon the *via negativa* is an expression of man's humble state: an expression that it is only by indirections that one can find directions out. (It is not irrelevant that Mr Eliot has quoted with approval the phrase in which the late Paul Elmer More claimed that Anglicanism is 'not compromise but direction'.) The marvellous achievement of *Ash-Wednesday* and the *Four Quartets* lies in their disclaimer of the possibility of human achievement and in their expression of a sense of waiting.

So when Mr Eliot opens *The Dry Salvages* with 'I do not know very much about gods', this suits well with the rest of the poem. But this makes it the more embarrassing when in some of his critical writing Mr Eliot by contrast seems to show such confident knowledge of the 'strange Gods' that his contemporaries go after. For the social criticism that results from this knowledge is rather superficial:

> And now you live dispersed on ribbon roads, and no man cares for his neighbour unless his neighbour makes too much disturbance, but all dash to and fro in motor cars, familiar with the roads and settled no-

where. Nor does the family even move about together, but every son would have his motor cycle, and daughters ride away on casual pillions.

I print this (unfairly) in prose, to show how close it comes to a paragraph from the Vicar's letter in the Parish Magazine. And further, the religious denunciations read sometimes likc those sermons about non-church-going preached fervently to the handful of goers.

> The country now is only fit for picnics. And the Church does not seem to be wanted in country or in suburb, and in the town only for important weddings . . .

or:

> Men have left GOD not for other gods, they say, but for no god; and this has never happened before that men both deny gods and worship gods, professing first Reason, and then Money, and Power, and what they call Life, or Race, or Dialectic . . . The Church is no longer regarded, not even opposed, and men have forgotten all gods except Usury, Lust and Power.

Yet perhaps it is unjust to quote exclusively from *The Rock*. And I think the trouble goes deeper. Celia, in *The Cocktail Party*, tries to explain her trouble to Sir Henry Harcourt-Reilly, and she says:

> Well, my bringing up was pretty conventional—I had always been taught to disbelieve in sin. Oh, I don't mean that it was ever mentioned! But anything wrong, from our point of view, was either bad form, or was psychological. And bad form always led to disaster because the people one knew disapproved of it. I don't worry much about form, myself—But when something's bad form, or mental kinks, you either become bad form, and cease to care, or else, if you care, you must be kinky.

Now I am not denying that this speech (and we know how glad Mr Eliot was when audiences took the verse of this play for prose) does represent a certain kind of young woman. And if she was to move from here to the kind of macabre destiny that Reilly and Mr Eliot designed for her, it was certainly at this point that her break had to come. I take it, too, that the slangy prose is designed to give us the young woman's awkwardness when having to discuss 'spiritual' matters: she is not slangy like this elsewhere, and evidently slips into

truer to say, she slips into (rhetorical) comedy

it here in the self-defensive way in which converts sometimes use provocatively bawdy language. Nevertheless, the passage still will not do. And it will not do because Mr Eliot is, too overtly, trying to gird at a generation, a civilization, through it. For the passage has somewhat the same satiric effect as the half-drunken apology of the knights after the murder of Becket: the satire, here and there, is clever and amusing—but perhaps basically lacking in charity to the victim. It is orthodox theology that we are all fallen. But the ruined millionaire deserves pity as well as laughter.

This is why I believe that the most profoundly religious elements in Mr Eliot's poetry lie in his oblique references to Man without God, or Man in Search of God. Perhaps even 'references' is too emphatic a word, for I mean the points at which Mr Eliot himself was probably least aware of the religious 'dimension'. And specifically I would locate them at the moments when he reveals a nostalgia for lost innocence. For what, at first sight, are children doing in the rose garden? Why do the *Four Quartets* ring with sounds of leaves

> full of children
> Hidden excitedly, containing laughter?

Or why does he ask (in 'A Cooking Egg')

> But where is the penny world I bought
> To eat with Pipin behind the screen?

The contrast (in *Burnt Norton*) between the shrieking voices

> Scolding, mocking, or merely chattering,

and the other noise:

> Even while the dust moves
> There rises the hidden laughter
> Of children in the foliage

is the contrast between the Waste Land and the Wonderland in which Alice moved and where laughter constantly lies beneath the solemn reflections. At the end of *Little Gidding*

> The voice of the hidden waterfall
> And the children in the apple-tree

are half-heard between two waves of the sea. And the rhythm of the river-god was, we remember, 'present in the nursery bedroom' (*The Dry Salvages*). Harry Monchensey, too, remembers how he came back for the holidays and tried to find the hollow tree where they had played at Injuns, but it had been felled and a summer-house erected 'to please the children'; and Agatha dared once to look through the little door when the sun was shining on the rose garden, and heard in the distance tiny voices—and then a black raven flew over. For Harry is her wished-for child, and a curse is like a child—but the curse will be ended by intercession, and Harry has found a clue in the children's treasure-hunt, a clue hidden in the obvious place. (I think that it is worth observing that the characters in *The Family Reunion* have a solid past: and this is one reason why this play is so immensely superior to the two which followed it, in which the characters have no past worth being interested in.)

The nostalgia for lost innocence emerges, of course, most clearly in Mr Eliot's Immortality Ode, which he called *Animula*. Dr E. S. Abbott once said that 'since we [adults] can no longer be Holy Innocents, there is only one alternative left to us—to become saints'. And this quest lies behind Mr Eliot's best poetry.

> Issues from the hand of God the simple soul

the poem begins. But then after 'moving between the legs of tables and chairs, rising or falling, grasping at kisses or toys', later comes the prison-house:

> The heavy burden of the growing soul
> Perplexes and offends more day by day.

And so now

> Issues from the hand of time the simple soul,
> Irresolute and selfish, misshapen, lame,
> Unable to fare forward or retreat.

Unable to fare forward: yet later, after the surrender and the discipline, Krishna (in *The Dry Salvages*) could give the command to 'Fare Forward' . . . After the expiation, the advance. However, this comes later, and even then is tentative. For the moment there is nothing but the consciousness of loss, the longing, and at best what would in a few years be called

> the barely prayable Prayer of the one Annunciation.

And so the last line of *Animula* can stand for much of the best of Mr Eliot's poetry, and for the profoundest sense in it of the supernatural, hinted at, longed for, recognized chiefly by its absence, by the wind that whistles round the fallen altars or the deserted chapel:

> Pray for us now and at the hour of our birth.

Onorate l'Altissimo Poeta

HUGO MANNING

If only one could call T. S. Eliot just a writer, not a poet. . . . I say this because the word poet sometimes touches off denigration and a wrong kind of awe. And it's the latter, I think, which is really pernicious; denigration is harmless, or at least far less harmful. Once, for example, I heard someone say poetry was trash and poets frauds or fools. A malicious, embittered person? No, an affable man who looked like Brassai's photo of a fat tuba player. And he seemed quite sincere when he added that poetry-writing was only forgivable in youth when one simply had to get all that nonsense out of one's system. It is better to be amused than shocked by such ignorance. Yet the bad thing about the other sort of ignorance—undeveloped or arrested taste—is that it treats *any* versifier as a poet. And that's how the power of differentiation is weakened, even lost—differentiation between poor dabblers in verse and those whose work has mastery and vision.

Differentiation, no doubt, should be sharpened and used as much as possible. Such a dynamic approach helps the cognition of those who come close to an ideal conception of a poet. And Eliot, I think, is a good example of such closeness. He strives for the maximum with the minimum. He is faithful to the struggle against obstacles to expression and vision: decaying definitions, unawareness and so on. But success is an illusion; the best to be hoped for is incomplete or temporary mastery when dealing with what Eliot calls the sleet and hail of verbal imprecisions. One remains acutely aware of the insufficiency of language even in Eliot's best poems which prod and produce, here and there, a conception of the inexpressible. Words crack and decay—he tells us in *Burnt Norton*—and only reach 'stillness' (the inexpressible?) by their form and pattern. How can one avoid seeing the attempt to make poetry as a sortie into the inexpressible with an ever-disintegrating machine? In poetry, I suppose, one must always chase after the possibility of the impossible.

Obviously dedication and the pursuit of some technical mastery—though vital in dealing with the tricky nature of words and idioms: the strangely vulnerable machine—are not enough. One must also consider the artist whose special style is felt in the form and pattern. For years I've tried to learn certain things about Eliot's art without much success. What makes his best poems so hypnotic yet inaccessible? Always they tantalize, and the feeling persists that one can't really possess them. The closer one comes to them the more their deepest secrets and meanings seem to retreat.

I'm only sure of this: that Eliot's art owes a lot to the way he unites the multi-dimensional. The spiritual and the somatic are well interwoven, and perhaps it's the representation of this polarity that gives so much life to his very best poems. And the reader's reaction? I've found that some people share, more or less, my own experience. Mind and senses are stirred, and there's a thrilling fusion of excitation and satisfaction. One also feels safe when trying to go with him on his special sortie. It's a welcome feeling, especially when one thinks of the let-downs by even clever poets. Thus what was meant to convey the transcendental becomes sloppy, even ridiculous; what was meant to represent song disintegrates into saccharine lyricism; and what was meant to give clarity to experience and the concrete becomes clogged with poeticity.

The word poeticity needs explaining. I don't know whether it exists, but I use it here to define glaring examples of verse imagery and rhetoric which don't pull their weight and give only an impression of 'poetry'. The word is meant to be contemptuous, but what contempt I feel for 'poeticists' is also levelled against myself for failures and misuse of the medium when trying to make poetry. Anyway, Eliot's value as a scavenger of poeticity shouldn't be under-estimated. He has uprooted some of the weeds of insensitive imagery, rejected or sharpened words which have lost clarity or become blunt, increased the power of definition and allowed sensuousness—in its most literal meaning—to breathe more freely within the suffocating limitations of language.

Eliot's representation of sensuousness makes me think of something George Santayana said about a taste for the world. In Eliot's case it is a taste which is *conveyed*, not hinted at, in his poems. His evocation of real things is sometimes electrifying, not necessarily because of descriptive precision. Perhaps the way he relates them to the abstract is one of the reasons for their special vividness. So withered stumps of time are told upon walls, damp souls of housemaids sprout despondently at area gates and dust in sunlight and memory in corners wait for the wind that chills towards the dead land. . . . The technical juxtaposition seems to point to a philosophical purpose: a firm acceptance of physical and spiritual, the indivisibility of all life, cesspit and temenos, Light Invisible and weeping multitudes. . . . This loyalty to what is and what is felt, to the somatic-sensuous and spiritual ideality, makes me think that Eliot's standpoint as an artist at least has some affinity with Kafka's belief that there is only a spiritual world, that what we call a physical world is the evil in the spiritual one and that what we call evil is only a necessary moment in our endless development.

The gist of some things Santayana wrote in his book *Three Philosophical Poets* has been at the back of my mind while writing this piece. Santayana spoke of a truly philosophical or comprehensive poet as one who could unite the insights of Lucretius, Dante and Goethe. (To him Lucretius was the poet of nature, Dante the poet of salvation, Goethe the poet of life.) He believed there were two directions in which the rational art of such a hypothetical poet should proceed; the first required great precision, justness and a taste for the world; the second required the expression of the ideal, thus using the outer life for the sake of the inner life, discipline for the sake of freedom, conquest for the sake of self-possession. Such a poet of 'double insight' should live in the continual presence of experience, should understand nature and have a delicate sense for the 'ideal echoes' of his passions. And then, like the poets in Dante's limbo, when Virgil returns among them, he can be saluted with the words *Onorate l'altissimo poeta*. Has any modern poet come closer to this creative synthesis than Eliot?

It's a good feeling to live at the same time as a great poet like Eliot, whose work is beautifu .and faithful, too. And if one is a Londoner that feeling should be enhanced. I think of Eliot as a Londoner, not as an American-born naturalized British subject. He seems as much a part of London, where he has worked so well, as its fogs and fountains, river-smells and gardens, hills of Hampstead, Ludgate and Putney, or *The Times* that issues from Printing House Square. . . . To conclude with an amendment of one of his own lines: 'How *pleasant* to meet Mr Eliot!—how very *pleasant* indeed!'

'Rose of Memory'

ISOBEL ENGLISH

WHEN I was sixteen, I had a friend—the brother of a girl with whom I had been at school—who lived in a basement in Charlotte Street. He had lately given up the job of publisher's reader in a family business and now lived on the dole which was then seventeen-and-sixpence a week. He also helped a couple of friends who were less fortunate than he.

In that basement I first made contact with the works of T. S. Eliot, where they took the place of a kind of Bible. Those strong slim volumes with their characteristic typography and rainbow jackets were the only concession to visible elegance amongst the dusty mattresses on the floor and the jam-pots to drink out of.

This was in the late 'thirties.

I can remember hearing the first few lines of *Ash-Wednesday* fall from the lips of my friend, and being pierced to the heart. The meaning was hidden from me, the submerged theme not then disclosed, but the words, the words on their own, were so separate and illuminating; solace for the struggling adolescence, a rod to fight with—even for such as I who did not partake as a true member and went home each evening to Kensington.

I used to copy out lines from *The Waste Land* on little slips of paper and leave them about my room, hoping that my parents would discover them:

> What are the roots that clutch, what branches grow
> Out of this stony rubbish?

I hated the Secretarial College to which I had lately been assigned, and I hoped that my family would question me about this poet who was adult and respectable and yet the word-giver of my friends whom they referred to as a *galère*.

'In this brief transit where dreams cross' what happened to time and the aggressive inclinations of the lately young? In the end it was the conforming exterior and diffident acceptance of everything that won. Like Mr Eliot's dictum, one found oneself at last sitting there 'serving tea to friends . . .'—in tea-cups. Basements were washed away in the war years and became broken-down warehouses or rat hide-outs; nobody lived there any more, or perhaps simply one did not know the people who did. My friend climbed out of the fields of conscientious objection that took him away in the war to a high desk in Whitehall that was neither better nor worse than his originally planned career in publishing, merely different.

We continued to be influenced, one could not avoid it when it had been so far beyond us at the moment of initiation; there was so much to catch up on. The works of T. S. Eliot became less of a Bible and more of the bread-and-butter of existence. One could not really 'hope to turn again'.

I once saw Mr Eliot at a gathering held to celebrate the twenty-first birthday of *Adam*, a literary magazine. He was pointed out to me. I saw him standing by a pillar in the midst of a vast throng who fluttered programmes for signature under his nose; with very little less discipline they might have attacked him, reverently, and torn out tufts of his hair. A 'lion' must be hunted while there are still lion-hunters to herd together, and there is still the scent. To become a disciple of a great master one has had to eat of his words; now it seemed one must also try to eat *him*.

Anatomist and Poet

JOHN ROSENBERG

SOMEONE like myself, without clear religious convictions, finds aspects of Mr Eliot's poetry beyond his reach. My approach is necessarily limited; but despite and within these limitations, his poems are affecting and profound in a particular way.

Social anatomist as well as poet, Mr Eliot takes as his starting-point human disillusionment, sterility and triviality. The disillusionment is that of rationalism, which has taught us to know God too little and ourselves too well.

Indications of his viewpoint are not far to seek in the poems themselves: as in *The Dry Salvages*, where he speaks of 'superficial notions of evolution'; or in *East Coker* ('... There is ... only a limited value / In the knowledge derived from experience. / The knowledge imposes a pattern, and falsifies.'); or, more strikingly, in the Choruses from *The Rock*:

> They constantly try to escape
> From the darkness outside and within
> By dreaming of systems so perfect that no one will need to be good.

'Darkness outside and within' is the picture. Hope itself is pointless, as we have no idea what to hope for.

At all events, the most sensitive among us, prone to psychology and temporization, are spiritual paralytics, our gaze turned inward on ourselves, precluding action and emotion. The soul grows

> Unable to fare forward or retreat,
> Fearing the warm reality, the offered good,
> Denying the importunity of the blood,
> Shadow of its own shadows, spectre in its own gloom.

The viewpoint is, of course, a religious one, and the poems are marked by it implicitly, too: the over-all cadence is invocatory as opposed to lyrical; the periods tend to be abruptly concise, theses rather than outpourings; the repetition at climactic moments is incantatory; there is frequent use of paradox.

Some of the poems are purely religious in tenor as well, and consequently not for all. The Choruses from *The Rock*, for example, point a religious way out of the blind alley. Men should cease to exist as humanly oriented individuals, and should become mere atoms in a sea of worship. Communal dedication should make their lives collective, like the act of building a temple, like the work of the anonymous builders of medieval churches. The requirement is self-negation, negation of all the self's complexities:

> A condition of complete simplicity
> (Costing not less than everything).

Those of us who lack Faith, and some who have it, cannot make such sacrifices: we find the implications of all communisms, even the spiritual one, appalling.

We may say that the business of art is either to inspire and renovate the soul, or to worship God, or possibly to do the one through the other; and that one of these functions is as good as the others.

But, it may be argued, spiritual renovation *per se* is no longer possible. It was all very well in the Nineteenth Century or before, when people believed in heroism, tragedy or the rational Enlightenment. However, as exemplified in Mr Eliot's work, we believe in these things no longer.

Scientific knowledge, mechanizing fact and truth, has stripped life of tragic possibilities and given it the flatter, fussier dimensions of comedy. Indicative of this are lines like those on the clairvoyante in *The Waste Land*, where the grim and terrible have to be punctured at regular intervals with banal comments:

> Had a bad cold.
>
> If you see dear Mrs Equitone,
> Tell her I bring the horoscope myself:
> One must be so careful these days.

The recurrent thread running through existence on the human level is triviality itself: 'I measure out my life with coffee spoons.' There is much tea-drinking and marmalade-eating in Mr Eliot's work.

And the concept of the heroic is no longer relevant, as we have become spectators and commentators, rather than actors in life.

> Am an attendant lord, one that will do
> To swell a progress, start a scene or two.

Our knowledge and our thinking impedes the life of the senses, too:

> I have lost my passion: why should I need to keep it
> Since what is kept must be adulterated?
> I have lost my sight, smell, hearing, taste and touch:
> How should I use them for your closer contact?

In this poem, *Gerontion*, the atrophy and emptiness of old age symbolize those in all life. Life gives only what cannot be accepted, through the gift being early, late or too much. What we have, finally, in place of the senses is 'a wilderness of mirrors'. Our withdrawal is well enough epitomized in the phrase 'go south in the winter'.

The romantic, too, comes in for its share of debunking. (See the early poem 'Burbank with a Baedeker: Bleistein with a Cigar'.) Disillusionment, triviality: what is most moving in Mr Eliot's work is that out of these unpromising facts of modern life he produces, conjurer-like, poetry and beauty. Investing human weakness and doubt with the sanctity of the Created, he *magnifies* them, in the sense in which we usually speak of 'magnifying God'.

> Will the veiled sister pray
> For children at the gate
> Who will not go away and cannot pray:
> Pray for those who chose and oppose.

The intellectual's faith, for all its agonized intention, must be imperfect. It is passages like this, not those on perfection and the 'building of the temple', that give the most inspiration, as their level is the common one of life's insolubility.

The Cultivation of Christmas Trees

D. E. S. MAXWELL

WHEN Mr Eliot abandoned the seeming nihilism of *The Waste Land* for his more overtly religious poems, he outraged many of his less perceptive admirers. In fact, his poetry has always been religious. Prufrock, Sweeney, Bleistein and the rest are creatures of a modern limbo, interesting to the poet because spiritually defective. Mr Eliot's early poetry is a deeply felt realization of a society indifferent to God, not a prolonged screech of ill-defined rancour. Reading *The Waste Land*, it was easy to identify it exclusively with the acutely observed contemporary drabness, the overpowering sense of a 'waste sad time'; and to forget that the poem focused on pilgrimage, an 'empty chapel', invited submission to 'controlling hands'. It is a poem not of assured disillusion—the fragments do remain to be 'shored against my ruins'—but, perhaps, of bewilderment, and from bewilderment there can be an issue.

There is, then, in the early poems, a conflict: between the poet's awareness of almost overwhelming spiritual disrepair in the world around him and his knowledge that this state of being can be properly evaluated not in its own terms, but only by standards which play no part in its fitful attempts to create 'systems so perfect that no one will need to be good'. Such a perception might indeed produce despair, but the despair need not be fruitless. One way to spiritual regeneration, to resolution of the conflict, is through a sense of 'the disorder, the meaninglessness, the mystery of life and suffering':

> Desiccation of the world of sense,
> Evacuation of the world of fancy,
> Inoperancy of the world of spirit;
> That is the one way . . .

—the dark night of the soul whose outcome may be 'ecstasy not of the flesh', spiritual revelation. This progress we witness in *Ash-Wednesday*, the Ariel poems and the *Four Quartets*, which contain Mr Eliot's most gravely moving verse. It is poetry of faith constantly in need of renewal, for which the one blinding moment of vision must be supplemented by 'prayer, observance, discipline, thought and action', in the words of *The Dry Salvages*.

So Mr Eliot's poetry is never one of easy affirmation. The Magi find their rebirth 'a hard and bitter agony', Simeon is denied 'the ultimate vision'; and in *Animula* the innocence of the child is prey to the corruption of the world. Passages in the *Four Quartets* do communicate perfectly the sublimity of revelation: the end of *Little Gidding* is a hymn to the ultimate harmony and concord of earthly life. But we are conscious always of the rigorous demands of religious discipline.

Since completing the Quartets, Mr Eliot has devoted himself largely to dramatic poetry, where he is concerned not with the intensity of personal vision, but with the conflicting visions of his characters. In *The Cocktail Party*, Celia chooses the way of sainthood, but the more mundane solution to the Chamberlaynes' problem is also acceptable:

> in a world of lunacy
> Violence, stupidity, greed . . . it is a good life.

This is in itself an answer to those who accuse Mr Eliot of lack of charity, and we may see something of the same spirit of acceptance in his latest non-dramatic poem, *The Cultivation of Christmas Trees*, his contribution to the series of Ariel poems published in 1954. In mood it is entirely different from the poems I have been discussing, the Quartets and inter-war series of Ariel poems, in which suffering is unequivocally the companion of faith. In this latest poem the mood is calm, assured. As in the earlier series of Ariel poems, the starting-point is the first Christmas, but this poem deals neither with the joy of revelation nor the agony of rebirth. It is a meditation on the symbolic value of the Christmas tree as seen by the child

> For whom the candle is a star, and the gilded angel
> Spreading its wings at the summit of the tree
> Is not only a decoration, but an angel.

Similarly, in *Animula*, also a poem about childhood, the child's world is one in which the untarnished imagination quickens spiritual perception. But in *Animula* the emphasis is on the dissolution of the child's purity of vision:

> The heavy burden of the growing soul
> Perplexes and offends more, day by day.

The Cultivation of Christmas Trees suggests that the 'spirit of wonder' may be sustained, so that, as life draws to its end,

> The accumulated memories of annual emotion
> May be concentrated into a great joy.

Simeon has 'eighty years and no to-morrow'. The 'eightieth Christmas' in the later poem preludes a joy which blends with and transmutes 'a great fear', the necessary human fear of death and judgment.

Inaugurated by the reference to St Lucy—to whom the children of Lombardy pray at Christmas for fulfilment of their wishes—the tone of this climax is solemn but unperturbed. It is the subdued, unobtrusive certainty, communicated partly by the relaxed verse, that seems new in Mr Eliot's verse, the almost playful association of the less elevated properties of Christmas—'the goose or turkey'—with the spiritual implications of the birth of Christ, 'when fear came upon every soul'. Such alignments of trivial and profound have, of course, been often used by Mr Eliot, but formerly the tone and the intention were ironic: 'I have measured out my life with coffee spoons'.

Here, in benign fellowship, the childish symbols are treated as entirely adequate to a more adult interpretation of the meaning of Christmas. We are past the agonized intensity of language and feeling in the other Ariel poems. *The Cultivation of Christmas Trees* is a flawless transcription of another kind of experience, the withdrawn peace of revelation assimilated.

T. S. Eliot the Londoner

JOHN BETJEMAN

THE yellow fog that rubs its back upon the window-panes may well have been a Boston fog, if they have them there: the four wax candles in the darkened room, which look to me so like somewhere in Bloomsbury (now bombed by Germans or demolished by London University), may well be in New England: the damp souls of housemaids sprouted for me at area gates in South Kensington, though New York may have been where the poet saw them: still I have the impression that Eliot is not only a town poet, but above all a London poet. Topography may not be an important element in a poem, there is little in Shelley, none in the seventeenth-century religious poems so much admired by Eliot, and yet London percolates most of his poems, and though he may call one *East Coker* and another *Burnt Norton*, London is in them both. Love of place may not be essential to the full enjoyment of his poetry, yet it is a noticeable part of it, especially love of London. It is a part of his character, too. A friend of mine recalls his saying 'Speaking precisely as an air-raid warden of South Kensington . . .'

He is associated in my mind very much with London. He is the first poet that I ever met. This was in 1916 when I was at Highgate Junior School and he was known there as the 'American Master'. He looked then very much as he does today and he spoke with the same slowness and exactitude. It was known among us then that he wrote poetry, although *Prufrock* did not appear until a year later.

A love for London starts with a feeling for the City which is the heart of London and its oldest part. No poet has described the smells and noises of the City of London so well as Eliot since the days of Langland and 'the London Lyckpenny'. I imagine Eliot getting out of the District Railway at Monument Station and seeing the crowds walking over London Bridge and joining them as he moves towards the Bank to where St Mary Woolnoth kept the hours. And in the lunch hour I see him walking down to look at the Thames at London Bridge and catching that smell of fish by Billingsgate.

> O City city, I can sometimes hear
> Beside a public bar in Lower Thames Street,
> The pleasant whining of a mandoline
> And a clatter and a chatter from within
> Where fishermen lounge at noon: where the walls
> Of Magnus Martyr hold
> Inexplicable splendour of Ionian white and gold.[1]

The City of London and its river are the chief topographical backgrounds to *The Waste Land.*

Eliot's love of London extends to the suburbs and home counties. His appreciation of Sherlock Holmes, that essentially London and Home County man, is largely concerned with those subtle details of Norwood, Reigate and Charing Cross which are part of the delight we have in the stories today. Addresses in London very much please Eliot. I remember his telling me how Miss Swan at Fabers, the publishers, of which he is a director, lived in Trossachs Road, Dulwich, and I remember the pleasure he had himself in living in Bina Gardens, S.W.5. Who but someone who had worked in the City as a clerk could have written:

> But where is the penny world I bought
> To eat with Pipit behind the screen?
> The red-eyed scavengers are creeping
> From Kentish Town and Golders Green.

And how well he understands the pathos of those thousands who droop in a hundred ABC's:

> Highbury bore me. Richmond and Kew
> Undid me.

The subtle class distinctions of outer London are in his poetry, too.

[1] He must have entered St Magnus not earlier than 1921, the year when the present rector, Fr. Fynes Clinton, was appointed. Before that St Magnus was low church, locked, box-pewed, dead and dusty. The Ionian white and gold must refer to the redecoration under Fr. Fynes Clinton by Martin Travers.

This quotation from *The Rock* is redolent of Esher and Wentworth.

> In the land of lobelias and tennis flannels
> The rabbit shall burrow and the thorn revisit,
> The nettle shall flourish on the gravel court
> And the wind shall say: 'Here were godless people:
> Their only monument the asphalt road
> And a thousand lost golf balls.'

Whether it is the public transport of London:

> Or as, when an underground train, in the tube, stops too long between stations
> And the conversation rises and slowly fades into silence
> And you see behind every face the mental emptiness deepen
> Leaving only the growing terror of nothing to think about;

or in what he loves best, the churches of our own beloved Church of England, it is London which inspires him, the London where he has lived for the last forty years:

> Ill done and undone,
> London so fair
> We will build London
> Bright in dark air,
> With new bricks and mortar
> Beside the Thames bord
> Queen of Island and Water,
> A House of our Lord.

W. B. Yeats and T. S. Eliot

G. S. FRASER

THE VIOLENT and precise gestures in words, the compelling images, the magisterial rhythms of these two great men have—I suppose I might quite honestly say—dominated my inner life since, among all the cloudy tensions of a provincial adolescence, I 'took to' poetry as in a Mediterranean society I might have taken to women, in Germany to metaphysics, in modern Asia to nationalistic politics. Yet, in taking to them both one was taking to opposites. Yeats's picture of Eliot, as late as the introduction to *The Oxford Book of Modern Verse*, was that of a satirist, painting life in cold, grey tones, only now and again, almost against the grain, producing a great romantic image; Eliot, as late as *After Strange Gods*, is extremely severe on Yeats for using magic as a kind of drug which, injected into its veins, will give a dying romantic tradition a spurious vitality. It would be interesting to know how often, if ever, on Yeats's visits to London the two men met and how, if at all, they got on.

I never met Yeats, and yet I feel I know him; I have met Mr Eliot and exchanged a word with him three or four times, and have heard him speak, or been in a room with him, more often than that; yet I do not feel, on the whole, that I know Mr Eliot. And there one gets a contrast that will help one in contrasting the poetry. Yeats is a poet like Donne or like Pope or like Byron whose material is to an extreme degree, at least in all his more mature and more lastingly impressive poems, his own experience of life, his own personal history, what he has seen, whom he has talked to, his lovers and his friends. As in Byron we can turn in Yeats from his poetry to his life, from his life to his poetry, and always rewardingly; for all the contrast that Yeats himself made between 'perfection in the life' and 'in the work', one's impression, retrospectively, is of unity between them;

of, in particular in the last twenty or so years of Yeats's life, the life getting, with enormous pressure, into the work and at the same time the work shaping the gestures, the manners, even the physical appearance of the man. In his youth Yeats looked a thin, willowy, droopy, floppy-tied bohemian, a perfect target for Sir Max Beerbohm; in his middle age, in the years when he was struggling to keep the Abbey Theatre going, he had a kind of heavy, cloudy handsomeness; there is a strange portrait of him by Augustus John at this period, that makes him, with an unshaven jowl and a sullen, thrusting jaw, look almost like a tramp; in his old age, he became as beautiful as an eagle. I have known, casually or intimately, an extraordinary number of poets in my lifetime, and very few of them—Empson, Kathleen Raine, Pablo Neruda perhaps do; Roy Campbell and Dylan Thomas perhaps did—in any sense satisfactorily, 'look the part'. Yeats did; Eliot does, but in quite another sort of way; and the similarity and the difference will prove relevant to my deeper theme.

Yeats did, as I say, and Eliot does 'look the part'; and there is a sense, of course, in which the outer aspects of Yeats as 'a sixty-year-old smiling public man', playing the Senator for all the part was worth, and the handsome Roman-American proconsular mask of Mr Eliot in his later years do make a subtly similar impression; the important difference is that Mr Eliot is not 'playing the part for all it's worth'; he *is* it. Neither in his life nor in his writing is Mr Eliot what Yeats, like Byron, always was: the poet as actor. (He is sometimes, at high moments and also at weak moments, the poet as preacher or orator: which Yeats never was.) There is a photograph (it was one of the best in Professor D. J. Gordon's recent striking exhibition, 'I, the poet William Yeats', at Reading University) of Yeats, in old age, broadcasting. He does not, I think, know that his photograph is being taken. He is addressing the microphone, literally addressing it; one hand, that not holding his script, slants sideways in a persuasive gesture; it seems to have been just ruffling his beautiful white hair; the eyes are sparkling, the lips are parted in a cajoling grin. It seems wrong of the microphone to remain so inanimate, so unresponsive. One sees the actor there, and the actor unbending:

one sees the roots of the actor's temperament, a childlike gaiety, a child's passion for pretending, for dressing-up: the love of illusion for its own sake:

> Players and painted stage took all my love,
> And not those things that they were emblems of.

One feels, on the other hand, in one's rare encounters with Mr Eliot, that he has not this temperament. There is a story of Yeats's being reproached by A. E. for the passion which he showed, at one time, for attending gay parties, for mixing in every sort of smart Dublin group. Yeats quoted (I think it was) Goethe: 'The poor *are*; the rich also are but they are permitted to *seem*.' The seemings of social life, the acts people put on, delighted him, and he thought of life also partly as the art of seeming. But Mr Eliot, when one is having a word with him over a glass of sherry, *is* and does not *seem* a 'public man'; it is rather as if Mr John Foster Dulles (to whom Mr Eliot bears a certain physical resemblance) were amiably relaxing, from the cares of State, to discuss literary amusements. There is a dry, sly, crackling American humour, a humour that sometimes fastens on something childish: 'Ah, Hamburger,' I heard him greet a younger poet, 'I have just been to Hamburg.' Or when, wishing to tell him that I had been trying to make some versions of Tibullus, I stumbled nervously over the Latin poet's name, 'I have never,' Mr Eliot remarked, 'heard of a poet of *that* name!'

That dry humour comes out too in his public lectures, it is like the sudden twinkle of grave eyes behind spectacles. But the humour seems to a casual acquaintance—I am not a personal friend of Mr Eliot's, and personal friends may have a different story to tell—a concession from behind impenetrable reserves. Is it that there is little to know, that Mr Eliot is of those who—as Gourmont, was it not? put it more or less about Flaubert—drain themselves away, squeeze themselves off, drop by drop, in their work? I cannot think so, for if a casual contact with Mr Eliot reveals immense reserves, it suggests also that they are reserves of power and of judgment: even five minutes confronted by his inscrutable courtesy can be an uncomfortable five minutes:

Reflected from my golden eye
The dullard knows that he is mad.
Tell me if I am not glad!

Here, perhaps, to sum all this—which is vague and tentative, which may seem too personal, but which is not, I think, irrelevant to criticism—to sum all this up, here, perhaps, we have a writer who combines a public spirit, a feeling that he must grace with his presence many public occasions, with either a natural vocation for solitude, an extreme fastidiousness about promiscuous sociability, or, simply, shyness. And a character like that has its obvious relevance to Mr Eliot's insistence, in his early critical writings, on the importance of *depersonalizing* the poetic art and the critical approach to poetry.

There are perhaps poets of whom it is true, in Mr Eliot's phrase, that for them 'poetry is not a turning loose of emotion, but the escape from emotion'. (Miss Kathleen Nott remarks about this passage: 'In the context Mr Eliot makes it clear that he finds it necessarily unpleasant to have emotions.') Indeed, for no poet, or for no artist of any kind, is poetry or any kind of art a 'turning *loose* of emotion'; but there are poets for whom poetry is very much an acting out the gesture of emotion, a kind of process that could be called, in a good and bad sense, self-dramatization.

Donne, Pope, Byron and Yeats, as I have already suggested, are four great self-dramatists. What Eliot dramatizes in early Browningesque poems like *Prufrock* and *Portrait of a Lady* is not himself but *personae*; and it is a mark of poets whose bent is towards this kind of other-dramatization that the shape of their poems will tend towards panorama, presentation, dialogue (that is the purely formal shape of *The Waste Land*, the shape of a radio feature for an impersonal narrator and a crowd of voices); the tendency of self-dramatization, in lyrical poetry, on the other hand, is towards soliloquy. (There is a sense in which Donne, Pope, Byron and Yeats are often doing what Mr Eliot has blamed Othello for doing in his last speech: 'cheering themselves up'.) The extreme importance of Browning as a source for a lot of both early Pound and early Eliot is now being widely recognized; and garrulous and buttonholing as Browning's style is, he is in the end a poet singularly reticent about his private emotions (and his personal life is not his material). His public personality again was notoriously not a 'poetic' personality, but that of a bustling, social diner-out. Dryden is another great poet whose poetry throws no light, does not derive from, a life whose purely personal emotions may not have been very interesting; and perhaps that was one reason why, in a famous early essay, Mr Eliot chose to pay 'homage' to Dryden rather than to his far greater, far subtler, far more intense, but also, of course, embarrassingly (from the point of view of a cult of depersonalization) more 'personal' successor, Pope.

Our portrait, then, of Mr Eliot as a poet is that of a young man whose natural bent was towards the dramatization of those aspects of his experience that he could make, as far as possible, objective; and who, if in his later poetry he turns towards the exploration of the self, or the exploration of conditions of order—or peace—in the self, does so in a way that is as far as possible from self-dramatization. The elements into which *Four Quartets* can be broken down, for instance, are exposition, presented scene, moral homily, celebratory lyric, poetic text and self-commentary, formal gesture of supplication—elements which have their analogues in the prayers, the hymns, the lessons, the text and sermon, the parting benediction of an Anglican church service, and not in Greek choruses or the great rants of the Elizabethan stage. For Mr Eliot *le moi est haïssable*, but can, and must, be set in order.

If Mr Eliot, in his later work, is typically at the lectern or in the pulpit or on his knees in the pew, Yeats is never off his own stage: 'Irving with his plume of pride'; and where Mr Eliot is his own congregation, Yeats is his own audience. Yeats was a shy man, too: but he described himself correctly, in a letter to Sturge Moore, as also being an 'extremely social man'. He was talking in that letter about his Nobel Prize, and saying that he cared more for what it meant to Ireland, a recognition of Irish literature by the world at large, than for what it meant to him; but I think he meant also that he was an extremely *sociable* man (it would be part of the touch of the lingering Eighteenth Century in his, and in Dublin's, idiom: as in the phrase 'a social glass'). Freud, it seems to me, was probably right in assuming that one of the material factors (as distinct from the *formal* factors, not as distinct from the *spiritual* factors) behind the acceptance, or the assumption, of the poetic calling is youthful loneliness, the sense of not being recognized. But there are those to whom recognition, the chance of making friends everywhere, that comes with poetic reputation—it can come, indeed, with quite minor poetic reputation—is still, in itself, delightful. And there are others to whom, when it does come, it has become an intrusion: to quote Yeats himself, on a different theme, but not inappositely:

> all triumph would
> But break upon his ghostly solitude.

For Mr Eliot perhaps the great world, when the world was at last at his feet, had become an intruder. But when one thinks of Yeats's attitude to the great world in every sense, one thinks first of the lines in 'The Municipal Gallery Revisited':

> You that would judge me, do not judge alone
> This book or that, come to this hallowed place
> Where my friends' portraits hang and look thereon;
> Ireland's history in their lineaments trace;
> Think where man's glory most begins and ends,
> And say my glory was I had such friends.

Yeats's attitude to people is essentially there. Those whom he loves he turns into myths; his poems are full of heroic profiles. But when I think of Mr Eliot's attitude to people (at its best and noblest), I think of the immense tired compassion of some passages from *The Waste Land*:

> My feet are at Moorgate, and my heart
> Under my feet. After the event
> He wept. He promised "a new start".
> I made no comment. What should I resent?
>
> On Margate Sands
> I can connect
> Nothing with nothing.
> My people humble people who expect
> Nothing.

When I think of Mr Eliot's attitude to people, on the other hand, at its less good and noble level, I think of a passion in the important early essay on 'The Function of Criticism' (the victim, the spokesman of the 'inner voice' who is being attacked, is Middleton Murry):

> My belief is that those who possess this inner voice are ready enough to hearken to it, and will hear no other. The inner voice sounds remarkably like an old principle which has been formulated by an elder critic in the now familiar phrase of 'doing as one likes'. The possessors of the inner voice ride ten in a compartment to a football match at Swansea, listening to the inner voice which breathes the eternal message of vanity, fear, and lust.

What is interesting there is the attitude to the common people, the specification, as particularly horrible, of those who ride in third-class carriages and go to watch football, a plebeian sport (and, perhaps, though of course people go a long way to watch football, are Welsh, not Anglo-Saxon, not members of the *Herrenvolk*). No doubt such people would be laughing and joking and showing off, and would have had a few drinks, and would be exchanging smoking-room stories; if the chattering counted as vanity, the bawdy jokes as lust, so no doubt the search for distraction—'distracted *from* distraction *by* distraction'—counted as fear. (And in the years after the First World War, when this essay was written, they would have plenty of things to be fearful about: their jobs, their wages, their families, their future.)

Yeats was ever so much more, in the romantic as well as the vulgar pejorative sense of the word, a 'reactionary' than Mr Eliot; what he really in his heart wanted back was the Ireland of Grattan's Parliament, an aristocratic republic with the Anglo-Irish gentry still in the saddle; he did not want what he got, a farmers' and shopkeepers' Roman Catholic democracy. But Yeats could never have been mean, snobbish and uncharitable about the common people, as Mr Eliot is in the passage of prose I have quoted (a passage written, of course, quite a number of years before his conversion to Anglicanism).

Yeats never really had to face the problem of what he felt about the industrial proletariat. There was not one, large enough to count, in Ireland. He was lucky to have been brought up in a society in which the two poles were still the gentry and the peasantry, not the owners and the hands; and that society shaped his social dream:

> John Synge, I and Augusta Gregory, thought
> All that we did, all that we said or sang
> Must come from contact with the soil, from that
> Contact everything Antaeus-like grew strong.
> We three alone in modern times had brought
> Everything down to that sole test again,
> Dream of the noble and the beggar man.

Or, earlier:

> We were the last romantics—chose for theme
> Traditional sanctity and loveliness;
> Whatever's written in what poet's name
> The book of the people.

For Eliot, on the other hand, there was no 'book of the people'. He started off as a man uprooted from urban civilization in one country to urban civilization in another; a middle-class mandarin, who saw in the modern industrial and commercial order (except in some aspects of it where something more gracious or more earthy lingered on—English public-houses and music-halls, for instance) merely the fragmentation, the grinding away of the organic life, of an older, firmer, sounder culture. It is out of such disgust that his social compassion comes (and he is a much more socially compassionate man than Yeats: is more of a man of his century than Yeats: is, in the teeth of his principles, in some ways, in some senses, in at least some shades of a nuance of these terms, a liberal and a humanitarian in spite of himself).

So it is useful to read Eliot, particularly Eliot up to *The Waste Land*, when one has become a little drugged with Yeats. Eliot turns one's eyes away from Lady Gregory and John Synge and the certainly in some degree imaginary or hopefully projected—'The strength that gives our blood and state magnanimity of its own desire'—loyalty and wisdom of the Kiltartan peasantry. Eliot, by contrast, perhaps paints too black. What is life like? It is, he seems to say, like Sweeney in and out of brothels: it is the typist and the carbuncular young man, it is drying combinations, upper-middle-class sexual neurosis, seductions on the river, abortions, despair.

The picture of disorder is just, as 'composed', as selective a picture as Yeats's 'dream of the noble and the beggar man'. Eliot himself said of *The Waste Land* that it expressed not a generation's disillusionment but its illusion of being disillusioned. We can see today, perhaps, that Yeats selected for celebration or idealization forces which, against whatever superficial discouragement, may have the power, after all, of perpetuating themselves; though it is not the idea which anybody officially defends or sets up as an alternative to Communism or the Big Business Society, one cannot say that the aristocratic ideal in Europe is dead. And, on the other side, Eliot's selectively damning picture of modern urban society remains *poetically* valid—though one no longer pretends that he is doing sociology in verse—because of the desperate compassion it engenders:

> I am moved by fancies that are curled
> Around these images, and cling:
> The notion of some infinitely gentle
> Infinitely suffering thing.
>
> Wipe your hand across your mouth, and laugh;
> The worlds revolve like ancient women
> Gathering fuel in vacant lots.

To go a little deeper: Eliot's world, his world of poetry, is what Gabriel Marcel calls a 'broken world': that is his topical significance for us—as apart from his permanent strictly poetic interest. But Yeats proudly and with a tragic gaiety transcends 'brokenness'. Let us take the notion at a level that (positively in Yeats, negatively in Eliot) is pretty near the centre for both poets: at the level of the paradoxes of sex, desire and revulsion, the holy and the obscene, the sacramental profanation. (It is the level of human experience at which, in a literal, a moral, an allegorical or anagogical sense, 'everything comes together'.) I think one is right in taking Eliot's

> The notion of some infinitely gentle
> Infinitely suffering thing

as an oblique reference to female patience under suffering; as that patience,

'What should I resent?'

'My people humble people who expect
Nothing',

is one of the redemptive values realized for us in *The Waste Land.* Here is Yeats, in the 'Crazy Jane' sequence, on a not basically dissimilar theme:

'A woman can be proud and stiff
When on love intent;
But Love has pitched his mansion in
The place of excrement;
For nothing can be sole or whole
That has not been rent.'

What has been rent is the hymen; a woman's parts are not 'sole or whole' till, in the act, she has lost her maidenhead and achieved her womanhood, has 'put on,' in John Donne's Aristotelian tag, 'perfection and a woman's name'. But Eliot has no gesture at all resembling this: throughout *The Waste Land*, male sexual aggression is something that women, far from being proudly and stiffly intent on, patiently—and passively—endure. It is their cross, their shame; it is in its intrinsic nature perhaps not only squalid but boring:

When lovely woman stoops to folly and
Paces about the room again, alone,
She smoothes her hair with automatic hand,
And puts a record on the gramophone.

It is a ticklish subject, full of rubs: but it does seem to me that it is Yeats, here, who is nearer central and traditional human feelings about love between men and women than Eliot. It would be an absurdity to say that Yeats's attitude to sexuality was orthodoxly Christian; but it was an attitude that is central and traditional even in Christian societies, since most Christians are sinners (which is what Christianity is about) and the Christian ideal of chastity is one that one man and woman out of ten thousand, or perhaps out of a hundred thousand, have the physique, the self-control or the special gift of grace to live up to. (This does not apply to the adoration of virginity: my friend Constantine Trypanis has written a beautiful dramatic poem, in which one of the key episodes is the worship, on the outskirts of her temple, by Chian prostitutes, of the chaste huntress, Artemis. It is those who have not been granted the grace of chastity who are perhaps especially drawn to adore virginity.) In relation to chastity and the Christian tradition, the Scottish poet, Tom Scott, has noted that Robert Burns's randiness, his genial general enthusiasm about 'the lasses', is not a reaction against Scottish Calvinism, but springs out of it: if most of us are going to be damned anyway—or if we shall be saved in the devil's teeth, through God's pure arbitrary mercy, in spite of our sins, since 'all our righteousness is filthy rags'—this is what is worth either getting by with or being damned for: 'Take what you want, said God, and pay for it.' Most people at some time or another in their lives *passionately* want this, and it is the lack of lucid understanding of or intuitive sympathy for such passion (it is the squirmy squeamishness), that is the great central gap in two such different poems of Mr Eliot's as *The Waste Land* and *Sweeney Agonistes.*

Both poems are extremely acute observations of man as a sexual animal (of more—of man as a spirit capable of damnation). But they are observations, not of the spirit capable of damnation, but of the sexual animal, from *the outside.* But is it natural to be on the outside? Mr Eliot was brought up, I believe, as an American Unitarian, the least innerly tense, I imagine, the most vapidly rational, the most gruel-like and digestible of faiths; but did he inherit from his remoter witch-hunting New England ancestors a kind of Manicheism, a kind of Puritan hatred and contempt for nature (a hatred which a poet like Mr Robert Graves might see as the expression of the desire of the human male—maleness being a symbol for will and intellect—to despise and dominate the human female—femaleness being a symbol for nature, for fecundity, nurture, all gentle consolations—on whom, in the long run, he utterly depends)? I do feel anyway that here, in this area, is the great lack or disbalance in Mr Eliot's achievement as a poet, in his embodying of the human condition. One thinks, in this connection, of James Boswell, as devout a Christian as Mr Eliot, who would never have scoffed at the Christian ideal of chastity, but who knew humbly that the weaker brethren—he and most of his neighbours—could not live up to it. Or I think of a Presbyterian, a Church of Scotland, joke, heard in Aberdeen in my youth: a crowd of the newly dead are queueing up outside St Peter's Gates; they are looking pretty glum; but a whisper runs from the head of the queue to the tail of it, and they cheer up: 'Fornication disna count, fornication disna count!'

I may have seemed dwelling too long, and perhaps in a slightly ribald manner, on the difference between Yeats's and Eliot's attitudes to 'the facts of life'. But what I have been saying is centrally important to my argument. If Yeats's poetic world could be 'broken', it would be as a hymen is broken, as a stage in the gaining of completeness; Eliot's early world—'real' or 'actual' world *and* poetic world—seems to me to have been broken like a bone: and in *Ash-Wednesday* and *Four Quartets* we can watch it slowly knitting up again. And part of the reason for the brokenness of Eliot's world was a rejecting attitude, a squeamishness about the natural order. Part of the reason, on the other hand, for Yeats's magnificent wholeness, all through, is what—not too flabbily, I hope—one can call an *accepting* attitude.

Yeats, of course, could rage:

> All day I'd looked in the face
> What I had hoped 'twould be
> To write for my own race
> And the reality;
> The living men that I hate,
> The dead man that I loved,
> The craven man in his seat,
> The insolent unreproved,
> And no knave brought to book
> Who has won a drunken cheer,
> The witty man and his joke
> Aimed at the commonest ear,
> The clever man who cries
> The catch-cries of the clown,
> The beating down of the wise
> And great art beaten down.

But that is a more generous rage, with worthier antagonists—is it not?—than Mr Eliot's youthful strictures on football excursionists in third-class railway carriages? And thinking of Eliot's early poetry —everything after *The Hollow Men* is different, not only in handling but in substance—one might, in some moods, half-agree with Yeats's verdict: 'Eliot has produced his great effect upon his generation because he has described men and women that get out of bed or into it from mere habit; in describing this life that has lost heart his own art seems grey, cold and dry.' And Yeats goes on (one doesn't at all agree with him that this is the only example in Eliot's early work of 'the grand style', though it is a striking one): I think of him as a satirist rather than a poet. Once only does that early work speak in the great manner:

> The host with someone indistinct
> Converses at the door apart,
> The nightingales are singing near
> The Convent of the Sacred Heart,
>
> And sang within the bloody wood
> When Agamemnon cried aloud,
> And let their liquid siftings fall
> To stain the stiff dishonoured shroud.

Sometimes, indeed, when I compare the early Eliot, the Eliot before *Ash-Wednesday*, and Yeats, I think of Shakespeare's Mark Antony and his Octavian: the grand squandering talent and the talent that never misses a trick. (And I think of Yeats's Dublin as being like Alexandria, in that it is not the centre, but it is lively, and of Eliot's London as being like Rome in that it is the centre, but is comparatively dull.) Mark Antony thought Octavian a cold fish, but was rightly afraid of him; when they fought battles together, Octavian gave the orders; when they played at dice, Octavian always won; and Antony could not make Octavian drink. No such comparisons go on all fours, but there is a real sense in which, in the 1920s and the 1930s, Eliot was a dominating influence on all the best new young poets—'a penetrating influence, like an East wind' as Empson describes him—and Yeats was a taste slightly to be apologized for. None of Eliot's major critical essays failed of the effect aimed at; it is due to him as much as to any other single man that a whole generation of readers exalted the Metaphysicals, yawned politely at the Romantics, were very well read in their Elizabethan dramatists, bracketed off Milton and so on. Yeats's critical remarks are often so fantastic, so much at the mercy of his fascination with special kinds of subject-matter, that no critic of the schools has, I think, noticed how unexpectedly magisterial some of his judgments—that on Pound in *The Oxford Book of Modern Verse*, for instance—are. He and Eliot were never drawn into any kind of direct controversy—their prose interests hardly at any point overlapped; if they had been, Yeats, like Mark Antony, would hardly have noticed if he had been defeated. As his correspondence with Sturge Moore about the existential status of hallucinatory cats shows, he was perfectly indifferent to being logically refuted in argument; he would stick to the position he had chosen and cajole, out of the air, a new defence for it.

Yeats, indeed, would never, like Mark Antony, have got drunk; he and Mrs Yeats celebrated his Nobel prize by frying sausages at midnight. But as he respected the mystery of desire, 'the fury and the mire of human veins', so he respected the mystery of drunkenness: in 'The Seven Sages':

> Whether they knew or not,
> Goldsmith and Burke, Swift and the Bishop of Cloyne
> All hated Whiggery; but what is Whiggery?
> A levelling, rancorous, rational sort of mind
> That never looked out of the eye of a saint
> Or out of a drunkard's eye.

What Yeats has to say about 'Whiggery' there may help one to bring out some contrasts between his attitude and Eliot's attitude—though both are 'reactionaries' in the common sense of the word—to politics.

Whiggery, in Yeats's use of the word, is not Whiggism (Burke, for instance, all his life could have called himself a Whig); Whiggism was a kind of aristocratic semi-republicanism, at once generous, militantly patriotic and, quite unconsciously, shockingly exclusive; it reserved the government of England for a network of great families, and for a few, a very few rich and talented *arrivistes*, like the elder Pitt, or brilliant hangers-on, like Burke (who never, however, got a place of real profit or power). But when Yeats denounced Whiggery he was thinking partly forward to Fox and the French Revolution, the left wing of the party who suddenly took their republicanism seriously, and partly backwards to Covenanters on a moor, bloody-minded 'Billy Boys', and of the whole pattern of eighteenth-century England's Venetian republic as coming ultimately out of 'Cromwell and his murderous crew'.

Yeats's own politics were not Whiggery, but in a way they were (as in his idealization of Burke and Grattan) not far from Whiggism; it is doubtful whether he could, in any real sense of the word, be called a Tory, as Mr Eliot has often called himself. There is an element of popularity, or of appeal to perhaps brutal and perhaps sensible popular prejudice, in all Toryism, and Yeats was lacking in that element: the mob for him was essentially—as when it tried to interfere with his putting on Synge and O'Casey at the Abbey Theatre—something to be defied. His nationalism was always, in a large sense of these words, full of liberality and humanity: of chivalry and compunction:

> Was it needless death after all?
> For England may keep faith
> For all that is done or said. . . .
>
> They must to keep their certainty accuse
> All that are different of a base intent. . . .
>
> We too had many pretty toys when young:
> A law indifferent to blame or praise,
> To bribe or threat; habits that made old wrong
> Melt down, as it were wax in the sun's rays. . . .
>
> We had fed the heart on fantasies,
> The heart's grown brutal from the fare;
> More substance in our enmities
> Than in our love: O honey-bees,
> Come build in the empty house of the stare.

Eliot rarely brings the substantial humanity of his politics into his poetry with this directness. We must catch, often, his political attitudes through an allusion:

Thinking of the key, each confirms a prison
Only at nightfall, aethereal rumours
Revive for a moment a broken Coriolanus.

The subject there is not directly politics but human isolation in the subjective self; that can be broken through only by the impulse to sympathize or the will to control; and we must, for the full impact of the proper name, have somewhere encapsulated in our memories the full impact of Shakespeare's play. Yeats, on the other hand, had the poetical good luck to be fairly near the practical centre, almost *at* the moral centre—

Did that play of mine send out
Certain men the English shot?—

of a sequence of events on a stage small enough to be envisaged by one spectator, a spectator at once tragically harrowed and ironically triumphant. (For the triumph of Irish political nationalism was, ironically, the death of the kind of Anglo-Irish cultural nationalism to which, battling for Synge and the Abbey Theatre, Yeats had for more than ten years given all his practical energies; it was a deadly blow to the 'big house' society to which Yeats looked for cultural leadership, for style in public life.) Eliot, contrastingly, was during and after the First World War, in that time of troubles, in London, in touch and yet out of touch with everything: an observer without power: his stage too glaring and too wide for one man's eyes to take in. Yet he takes in something: here, in *The Waste Land*, he seems to prophesy the Second World War and its consequences:

What is that sound high in the air
Murmur of maternal lamentation
Who are those hooded hordes swarming
Over endless plains, stumbling in cracked earth
Ringed by the flat horizon only
What is the city over the mountains
Cracks and reforms and bursts in the violet air
Falling towers
Jerusalem Athens Alexandria
Vienna London
Unreal.

'Unreal': that is a word to pounce on there, an Eliotic and non-Yeatsian word, a word that can help us to specify a fundamental difference. Everything for Yeats *was* real. He used G. E. Moore's famous 'Refutation of Idealism'—the argument, roughly, that what is private to each of us as a sensing being, the colour blue on a perceived shaped surface, say, is not mental or subjective, is not a *blue sensation*, but is an objective *sensation of blue*—to support his belief that the hallucinatory cat which Ruskin threw out of a window was quite as 'real' as any actual cat which Ruskin, being a humane man, would never have thrown out of the window at all. Hallucinations as much as actualities come, for Yeats, out of a common stockpot which we can quite indifferently call Reality or Mind.

Eliot, on the other hand, in his concern with the feeling of unreality, was on to something subtler: the sense of gap, blank, hollowness, nausea in everyday life: the sense that the so-called humanly existent is sometimes the floppiest, flabbiest, most incoherent of day-to-day improvisations. He is saying often in his earliest poems particularly that actual life is unreal because it seems to consist of layers and layers of absurd pretension or pathetic misapprehension: and that 'real' life, say, would be like a boy's adventure story, like swinging a cutlass in the hot rains: or would be something subhuman, submerged, fierce, instinctive:

> I should have been a pair of ragged claws
> Scuttling across the floors of silent seas,

or legendary, sirenic:

> We have lingered in the chambers of the sea
> By sea-girls wreathed with seaweed red and brown
> Till human voices wake us and we drown.

And the feeling of the unreality of the actual persists in the later, profounder poems, though reality is no longer thought of as the life of a lobster or the embrace of a mermaid; and unreality is seen, now, less as a vacuum than as a kind of protection:

> Yet the enchainment of past and future
> Woven in the weakness of the changing body,
> Protects mankind from heaven and damnation
> Which flesh cannot endure.

In these contrasting attitudes to reality one comes, I think, on the profoundest antithesis between Eliot and Yeats; and one understands why, being opposite, they are also complementary. Eliot is a Christian, Yeats was not; it is hard to define exactly *what* Yeats was, but it is not wholly misleading to say that he was a spiritual pluralist of the type of McTaggart and also that he believed in some kind of reincarnation, and that in some, though not all, of his moods he welcomed the idea of reincarnation; but one should also remember that his mind was in some ways a much more playful mind than Eliot's and that he offers us *A Vision*, for instance, not as a doctrine but as a schema; he does not bother much whether we 'believe' it or not, or whether he himself does; as it has helped him to write his poems, it will help him and ourselves to understand them.

I think the best way of understanding Yeats's attitude to ideas (and I fancy it is an attitude that Eliot himself finds very difficult to understand) is to imagine a dreamy and imaginative schoolboy, who has read widely but in a dipping, unsystematic way, being given a lecture, say, either on Great Religions of the World or Great Philosophies of the World. He does not seem to have been attending much, so his teacher says: 'Now, to show me that you have understood, please write me a short essay, constructing either an *imaginary* great philosophy or an *imaginary* great religion.' Yeats would have done this like a shot: he missed the point of *real* philosophers, like G. E. Moore, for instance, because he could not imagine that they could be so pernicketily concerned with such very prosaic questions. As an imaginary great philosophy, I think *A Vision* is a very good book, indeed; so, as an imaginary great religion—but not quite so imaginary, for in a sense Yeats lived by it—the 'religion of poetry' which Yeats made up for himself out of legends, pictures, hocus-pocus and any handy picturesque odds and ends, in his youth, so is that also a very good religion. We must think of Yeats, in fact, as looking on religion and philosophy both, in the ordinary man's sense of these terms, from the outside, with the curiosity of an artist: not asking, 'Is this valid?' or 'Is this true?' but either, 'How does this help me as a poet?' or 'How does this look, in itself, as a work of human art?'

In the phrases of Yeats's own system, Yeats's type of poetic mind is subjective or antithetical: Eliot's is objective or primary. Eliot feels that he is checked, thwarted, controlled or led on by a reality (or a Reality) outside himself. For Yeats there is not really a world outside himself, for time and space and the visible world are merely the means by which, in a kind of play (in the sense both of drama and pastime) spirits both make themselves present to and disguise themselves from each other, the stage of a perpetual redemptive metamorphosis. And as doctors talk about a self-healing power in nature, so Yeats believed that there is a self-healing power in spirit:

> Considering that, all hatred driven hence,
> The soul recovers radical innocence
> And learns at last that it is self-delighting,
> Self-appeasing, self-affrighting,
> And that its own sweet will is Heaven's will.

Contrast such a passage with the terrifying specification, in *Little Gidding*, of 'the gifts reserved for age':

> 'the shame
> Of motives late revealed, and the awareness
> Of things ill done and done to others' harm
> Which once you took for exercise of virtue.
> Then fools' approval stings, and honour stains.
> From wrong to wrong the exasperated spirit
> Proceeds, unless restored by that refining fire
> Where you must move in measure, like a dancer.'

The spirit for Mr Eliot is *not* 'self-delighting, self-appeasing, self-affrighting'. It is not so easy to 'drive all hatred hence'. The difference between Heaven's will and the soul's own sweet will—but Mr Eliot would put the pair the other way round—is not a gap which is really an illusion: it is a gulf the crossing of which may take a lifetime's pilgrimage, 'costing not less than everything'. Thus Mr Eliot's great gift is a gift chastened, as it were, by at first an awful sense (like Sartre's nausea and Kierkegaard's dread) of the unreality of the actual; and then by an acceptance, slow, hesitant and painful, of the way of renunciation. Yeats's great gift is a gift unchastened, unchristened, unappalled:

> Does the imagination dwell the most
> Upon a woman won or woman lost?
> If on the lost, admit you turned aside
> From a great labyrinth out of pride,
> Cowardice, some silly over-subtle thought
> Or anything called conscience once;
> And that if memory recur, the sun's
> Under eclipse and the day blotted out.
>
> Man is in love and loves what vanishes.
> What more is there to say?
>
> . . . When we were young
> We loved each other and were ignorant.

Neither Mr Eliot's Christian morals now, nor perhaps his appreciation of life at any time, would have permitted him to say such things. Yet this unregenerate, this self-absolving voice, is the natural voice of poetry; it finds its echo at once in something wild and deep in the human heart. Mr Eliot's later poetry, which is also his greater poetry, finds its echo especially in the hearts of those who have walked some way on a path like his own of purgation. We feel that the two great poets are complementary because we sense obscurely that there is some point at which the way of acceptance and the way of rejection of the world's bright images meet. I am not talking mystically, but still as a literary critic: I think Yeats indicated where the point is when he said:

> Now that my ladder's gone,
> I must lie down where all the ladders start
> In the foul rag-and-bone shop of the heart.

I think Eliot indicated it also in some of his lines that move me most deeply:

> And the lost heart stiffens and rejoices
> In the lost lilac and the lost sea voices
> And the weak spirit quickens to rebel
> For the bent golden-rod and the lost sea smell

Quickens to recover
The cry of quail and the whirling plover
And the blind eye creates
The empty forms between the ivory gates
And smell renews the salt savour of the sandy earth.

Great poetry is what it is because it makes living, permanent and enriching order out of the heart's need, the heart's clamour for joy: which is also, alas, the heart's certainty of confronting pain.

Index of Plays, Poetry and Prose

PLAYS

POETRY

PROSE

Index of Names